# Reader's Digest
# Household
# Maintenance
# & Repair
## Manual

# Reader's Digest
# Household
# Maintenance
# & Repair
## Manual

## Expert guidance on maintenance and repairs in the home

Published by
The Reader's Digest Association Limited
London • New York • Sydney • Montreal

# Contents

## Introduction

6    When things go wrong
10    Basic toolkit
16    Safety in the home


## Around the house

20    The electrical system
22    The consumer unit
24    Fitting a new plug
26    Socket outlets
28    Replacing lights and switches

30    The water system
34    Taps
40    Toilets
46    Electric shower
48    Waste water problems
52    Central heating
58    Immersion heater

Locks
60    Cylinder door lock
62    Mortise door lock


## Appliances

Washing and drying
66    Washing machine
71    Tumble-dryer

Kitchen appliances
74    Fridge-freezer
77    Dishwasher
80    Ovens and hobs
82    Cooker hood

84 Small appliances
Food processor, Electric kettle, Iron,
Filter coffee maker, Toaster
90 Vacuum cleaner
94 Electric heaters
96 Extractor fan

# Audio-visual, computing and communications

Sound systems
100 Compact disc player
101 Record deck
102 Cassette deck
104 Amplifier
105 Loudspeaker

Television and audio
106 Television set
108 Video recorder
110 Audio-visual connecting leads
111 Remote control
112 DVD player
114 Satellite decoder

Computers
116 Keyboard
117 Mouse
118 Printers
120 Computer connecting leads

Communications
122 Telephone wiring

124 **Useful contacts**

125 **Index**
128 **Acknowledgments**

# Finding fault with the electrical system

Your electrical system can fail at several different levels. The cause may be something as simple as a blown plug fuse or faulty appliance, or there may be a fault in your circuit wiring. Follow the flow chart below to help you to diagnose the problem and work out how to fix it.

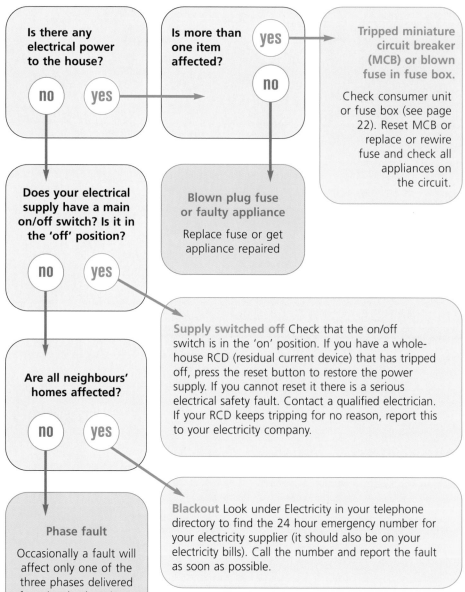

**Is there any electrical power to the house?**

no    yes

**Is more than one item affected?**

yes    no

**Tripped miniature circuit breaker (MCB) or blown fuse in fuse box.**

Check consumer unit or fuse box (see page 22). Reset MCB or replace or rewire fuse and check all appliances on the circuit.

**Does your electrical supply have a main on/off switch? Is it in the 'off' position?**

no    yes

**Blown plug fuse or faulty appliance**

Replace fuse or get appliance repaired

**Are all neighbours' homes affected?**

no    yes

**Supply switched off** Check that the on/off switch is in the 'on' position. If you have a whole-house RCD (residual current device) that has tripped off, press the reset button to restore the power supply. If you cannot reset it there is a serious electrical safety fault. Contact a qualified electrician. If your RCD keeps tripping for no reason, report this to your electricity company.

**Phase fault**

Occasionally a fault will affect only one of the three phases delivered from local substations, so power continues to be supplied to some neighbouring houses. Call the emergency number of your electricity supplier and report the fault.

**Blackout** Look under Electricity in your telephone directory to find the 24 hour emergency number for your electricity supplier (it should also be on your electricity bills). Call the number and report the fault as soon as possible.

## ELECTRICAL EMERGENCY ACTION

■ If anyone receives a minor shock from an appliance, stop using it and have it checked by an expert.
■ If someone receives a major shock, turn off the current immediately at the consumer unit. Refer to the guidelines on pages 22–23.

# Faulty appliances

Even if you don't want to do a repair yourself, working out why an appliance is not working will equip you to brief a professional and anticipate his recommendations, saving time and money. Remember that DIY repairs may invalidate a warranty.

## Assessing the fault

### Operator failure
Always read the instructions. Don't assume that a new appliance will work in the same way as the old one it's replacing.

### Mechanical failure
Often items stop working for very simple reasons: moving parts become jammed; drive belts slip off their pulleys; a door or lid may not have been closed properly. On some electrical equipment, a cut-out may have operated to protect the machine from overheating or overloading and this may need resetting.

## Decide what to do next
Consider how complicated the repair is and whether you think you can fix it yourself. Weigh up how urgent it is, how much you are prepared to pay for someone else to tackle the problem and whether repair is a feasible or economic option. It may be simpler and cheaper to buy a replacement.

### Is the appliance under warranty?
Any goods that develop a fault within 28 days of purchase should be returned to the place where they were bought, where you are entitled to a replacement or refund. Even outside this period many retailers will agree to replace or refund faulty goods. Most new equipment is guaranteed against parts failure for at least a year. Trying your own repairs may invalidate the guarantee, leaving you with an expensive repair bill if you fail to put things right yourself.

### Can you fix it yourself?
This book will help you to diagnose and tackle faults with individual systems or pieces of equipment. By explaining what is involved in the tasks, it will also enable you to decide whether your skills are up to the job, and to check whether you have the necessary tools and equipment.

### Do you need a professional?
Complex tasks and faults with expensive major appliances may call for professional repair. If tackling a particular job requires the purchase of several expensive tools you may never use again, the case for calling in a professional becomes stronger.

## Calling the professionals
If you cannot get a faulty appliance replaced, you have three repair options: the manufacturer; an independent repair agent or an electrical retailer. Note down the make and model of the appliance and a summary of the problem. Confirm the hourly rate for the work and whether there is a call-out charge and once the fault has been diagnosed, ask for a written quotation for the repair before work starts.

### Manufacturers and appointed agents
If your appliance is still under warranty, consult the instruction book or contact the manufacturer for the name of an approved repair agent.

### Independent repairers
These will tackle general repairs to most makes of appliance. You will find them listed in your telephone directory under Electrical Appliance Repairs.

### Electrical appliance retailers
Some retailers run their own service departments and may be prepared to repair appliances bought elsewhere.

## Safe disposal
Before you throw away any item, check that it is safe to dispose of, and that there are no recycling or recovery schemes in operation in your area.

A small appliance is likely to end up in the dustbin with other domestic rubbish and could cause harm to anyone who finds it and tries to use it. Cut off the flex close to the appliance to render it harmless then bend the plug pins with a hammer so that the severed flex cannot be plugged in. Alternatively, you could contact an organisation such as Waste Watch for details of schemes in your area that accept basic electrical equipment for repair and re-use by low-income households.

Larger appliances need to be safely disposed of – especially if, like fridges and freezers, they contain dangerous chemicals. Your local waste authority is obliged to accept unwanted appliances free of charge, if you can take them to an approved waste site, or for a small fee for collection.

WHEN THINGS GO WRONG

# Common plumbing and

## The plumbing system

Your plumbing system can suffer from a wide range of faults, but they fall into four main categories.

### Taps and valves ❶

Taps and valves control the flow of water into the home. They may drip, jam open or closed, or become hard to operate. The rising main stoptap (right) controls the flow of water into the house. It supplies the hot and cold water storage tanks, the kitchen cold tap and some appliances, such as a washing machine. The rising main can be drained via the drain valve, which is usually near the stoptap. Attach a length of hosepipe to direct the water out of doors.

### Supply pipes ❷

Supply pipes distribute water to wherever it is needed. They may leak, due to holes in the pipe or faulty seals at joints. They

---

> **PLUMBING EMERGENCY ACTION**
>
> ■ If a fault causes water to escape, aim to stop the flow as quickly as possible.
> ■ Make sure you know in advance where the rising main stoptap is located and that it turns on and off freely.
> ■ Empty leaking water storage tanks and supply pipes by turning off the main stoptap and opening cold taps, or by attaching a garden hose to a drain valve and opening the valve with pliers or a spanner.

---

may also become blocked by limescale. Leaks demand swift damage limitation – *see* Plumbing emergency action (above).

### Storage tanks ❸

Storage tanks hold cold and hot water. They may develop leaks or, in the case of the hot tank, may become inefficient due to a build-up of limescale. Replacement is the only long-term solution. There may be an on/off valve on the supply pipe leading from the cold water storage tank. In the event of a leak from one of these pipes, turn off the valve and open all the cold taps to empty the pipes. If there is no valve coming out of the tank turn off the rising main stoptap (above left) and open all the taps to drain the tank.

If the hot water cylinder develops a leak, the cylinder must be emptied by attaching a length of garden hose to the drain valve close to its base and opening the valve. Turn off the supply to the cylinder or empty the cold water storage tank too (see above). Opening hot taps will not drain the cylinder.

### Waste pipes

Waste pipes convey used water from appliances and WCs to the household drains, via U-shaped traps designed to keep drain smells out of the house. They can become blocked, causing overflows, but most blockages can be cleared easily by dismantling, plunging or rodding.

# heating faults

## The heating system

A central heating system consists of five main components, each of which can malfunction or fail.

### The boiler ❶

The boiler heats the system (and may also provide domestic hot water). It contains a number of parts that will need regular maintenance and eventual replacement and this is a job for a professional. For any work involving gas pipework, it is a legal requirement that the fitter is registered with the Council for Registered Gas Installers (CORGI). Annual servicing will keep the boiler in good order.

### The pump ❷

The pump circulates heated water round the system. It may become jammed or noisy or may fail altogether. Regular operation and cleaning help to prevent problems, but replacement is usually straightforward.

### The radiators ❸

The radiators transmit heat to individual rooms. They sometimes develop pinhole leaks due to corrosion, and may trap air, gas or sludge (by-products of corrosion), all of which can cause uneven heating or banging noises when in use. Using a corrosion inhibitor or leak sealer will help to prevent or cure these problems. Leaks require prompt action.

### The header tank ❹

The header tank (also called the feed-and-expansion tank) tops up any water lost from the heating system through leaks or evaporation. The tank itself may also develop a leak and need replacing. The ballvalve that refills it may jam through lack of use, causing an overflow or allowing air to be drawn into the radiators and pump. A ballvalve can be repaired or replaced. If the heating system develops a leak, turn off the boiler and drain the system using the drain valve at the lowest point, often at the front of the house.

### The controls ❺

Controls operating the heating system include a programmer, thermostats and motorised valves. They may fail through faulty wiring or mechanical failure.

---

**HEATING EMERGENCY ACTION**

■ If the system overheats or the pump fails, turn off the boiler.
■ Turn off the gas at the meter immediately if you smell a gas leak and call the Transco gas emergency number (0800 111 999).
■ Until you can make a repair, drain leaking pipes, radiators and hot water cylinders via the relevant drain valve.

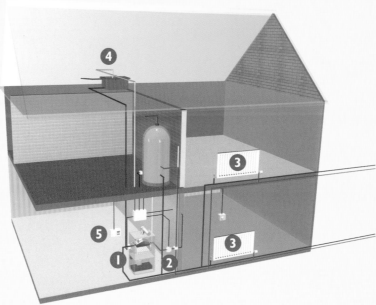

WHEN THINGS GO WRONG

# Basic toolkit

Many of the step-by-step repair procedures listed in this book require the use of tools. There will be occasions when you may need to hire or purchase a specialist tool, but the following basic items should be in every well-equipped toolbox.

## Organising your toolkit

Most modern toolboxes have multiple stacking layers. Put tools to which you need quick access in the top layer. It is sensible to put cutting tools, such as junior hacksaws and retractable blade knives, in the second layer where they are safely out of the way but not loose in the base of the toolbox. Oils and liquids should be stored in the bottom layer, in case they leak.

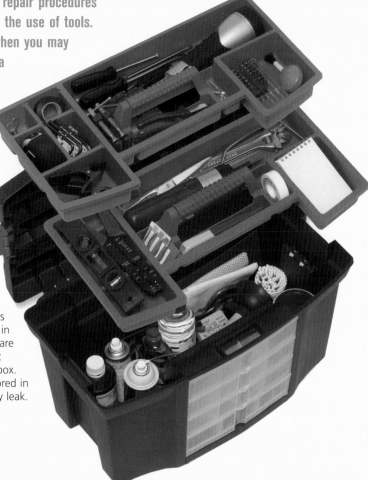

## Cutting tools

Always keep blades retracted and hinged cutters closed for storage.
**Knife** A retractable blade knife with replaceable blades is a highly versatile tool.
**Cutting mat** For safety, it is worth investing in an A4 size or larger cutting mat. Using this prevents a knife blade from slipping as you cut.

**Junior hacksaw** For small jobs, such as cutting through wood or metal, a cheap junior hacksaw is ideal. Because the thin blades are prone to snapping, they are easily replaceable.
**Scissors** A pair of general purpose scissors will also be useful to have at hand.

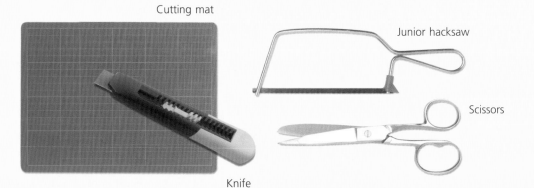

Cutting mat

Junior hacksaw

Scissors

Knife

# Screwing, unscrewing and holding tools

These are probably the tools that you'll use most often, so they should be made easily accessible. Ensure that screwdrivers are kept in their sets so that you can readily select the correct size and tip for the job.

**Flat tip screwdrivers** These fit into screws with a single slot head.

**Phillips and Pozidriv screwdrivers** A cross tip makes these safer than flat tip screwdrivers as they are less likely to slip under pressure. You will need to have at least one small and one medium-sized driver of each type.

**Hexagon keys** A selection of different sizes is useful for undoing hex-head screws.

**Watchmaker's screwdrivers** A set of tiny screwdrivers, providing a variety of Phillips and flat tips, is useful when working on small appliances.

**Socket set** For undoing and tightening small nuts and bolts, sockets are ideal.

**Long-nosed pliers** A slender tip is perfect for gripping small items and for bending wire objects.

**Clamps** A set of clamps can be useful for securing items to a work surface or holding glued things together while the glue dries.

Flat tip screwdrivers

Pozidriv screwdrivers

Phillips screwdrivers

Hexagon keys

Watchmaker's screwdrivers

Long-nosed pliers

Clamps

Socket set

# Measuring tools

If you want professional DIY results, you'll need tools to help you to measure accurately. It is always wise to keep a pencil and paper in your toolbox, where it will be at hand when you need it.

**Steel ruler** This is a sturdy guide for cutting and drawing and is useful for measuring too.

**Retractable steel tape measures** These come in a variety of lengths, with a lock button that keeps the tape extended when measuring.

**Spirit level** An invaluable tool when installing items such as dishwashers that must be level – the longer the better, for accurate levelling.

**Notepad and pencil** When attempting any repair project it is a good idea to have something for jotting down measurements or drawing diagrams of components and connections to aid with reassembly of an item you are taking apart.

**Plain white labels** When dismantling appliances, these are useful for labelling parts and wires so that you know how to reassemble them.

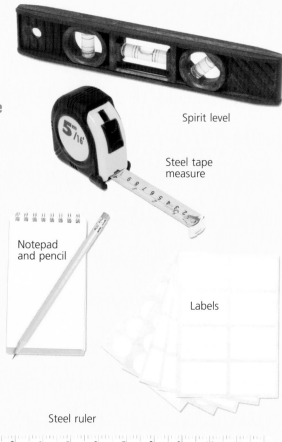

Spirit level

Steel tape measure

Notepad and pencil

Labels

Steel ruler

# Plumbing tools

These often get wet during use, so always dry them before replacing in the toolbox.

**PTFE tape** This thin, plastic tape is used for sealing threaded joints in plumbing, such as compression fittings and radiator connections.

**Radiator key** Radiators need bleeding from time to time to release a build-up of air that will reduce their efficiency. Some bleed keys have built-in drip catchers.

**Adjustable spanner** A versatile tool, allowing you to turn nuts of various different sizes.

**Stilson wrench** Use this with an adjustable spanner to prevent pipes, valves or taps from twisting when undoing nuts.

**Plunger** Can help clear blockages in pipes and plugholes.

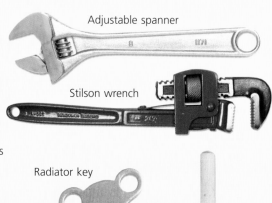

Adjustable spanner

Stilson wrench

Radiator key

Plunger

PTFE tape

# Electrical tools

The contents of this section of the toolbox range from small plug fuses to large torches and rolls of tape. Make sure you are fully familiar with where everything is: you'll want to be able to find the torch easily, should the lights fail.

**Fuse wire** Necessary only if your house has an old-style fuse box. Make sure you have spare wire for all the common ratings.

**Plug fuses** These should blow before the fuse in the fuse box or the miniature circuit breaker (MCB) in the consumer unit. Household appliances need a 3A, 5A or 13A fuse, depending on their wattage. Keep spares of each and always replace a blown fuse with one of the same rating.

**Socket tester** Plug this into socket outlets to test if they are wired correctly and safe to use.

**Red or brown PVC insulating tape** Useful for temporary repairs to damaged flex, and for identifying live cores in household wiring.

**RCD adaptor** Cuts the supply of electricity to an appliance if you touch a live part, offering extra protection against electrocution. Always use one when working with electricity outdoors.

**Torch** Invaluable in a power cut. Check the batteries regularly and keep a spare set in the toolbox.

**Wire strippers** Use the larger hole to cut through flex sheaths; the smaller hole to remove the plastic insulation from around the cores; and the sharp blades to cut through the core.

**Wire cutters** Useful to have at hand for cutting cable and snipping cores.

**Cable detector** Before drilling into walls, use one of these to check for concealed cables and water pipes.

**Multimeter** Lets you check the current and voltage flowing through electrical devices, simply by placing its probes on any two exposed contact points. It can also be used to check continuity – whether there is an electrical connection between two points.

**Inspection lamp** Useful when working on lighting circuits, or when doing repair work in any awkward-to-reach or unlit spots, such as the loft.

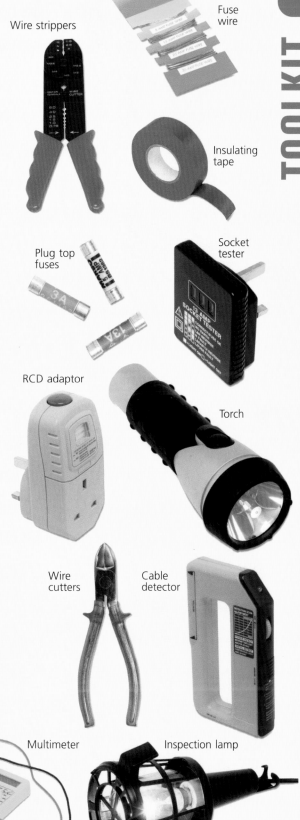

Wire strippers

Fuse wire

Insulating tape

Plug top fuses

Socket tester

RCD adaptor

Torch

Wire cutters

Cable detector

Multimeter

Inspection lamp

# Lubrication and water repellents

Use the right lubricant to keep appliances, tools and machines running smoothly.
To avoid spillages in your toolbox, make sure all lids are replaced firmly.

**Light machine oil** Often referred to as 'three-in-one' or 'multipurpose' oil, this is usually supplied in plastic or metal canisters, about the same size and shape as lighter fluid containers.
**Aerosol water repellent** (WD40) This light oil can be sprayed on for lubrication and for repelling water from electrical contacts.

Aerosol
water
repellent

Light
machine oil
(Three-in-one)

# Cleaning materials

**Appliances that are kept free from dirt and dust will last longer. Flammable solvents should be stored outdoors.**

**Lint-free cloths** Useful for applying cleaning agents such as isopropyl alcohol.
**Disposable household cloths** Use these when cleaning with water and mild detergent.
**Air blowers** Sometimes sold as 'lens cleaners' in photographic shops, these are small bellows with brush tips for dusting and blowing away small particles.
**Aerosol air duster** For more powerful dust removal. A jet of air can remove dust from areas that a cloth or cotton bud cannot reach.
**Isopropyl alcohol** An effective cleaning agent for electrical contacts. It is highly flammable.
**Wet-and-dry abrasive paper** For cleaning, smoothing and preparing surfaces.
**Switch cleaner** Used to clean inaccessible switches, such as the volume controls in audio systems.
**Washing-up liquid** When diluted it makes a gentle but effective cleaning agent.
**Cotton buds** Perfect for cleaning components in hard-to-reach places: look out for lint-free ones.
**White spirit** A highly flammable liquid that should be stored safely. It can be used for removing grease.

Aerosol air duster

Air
blower

Cloths

Switch
cleaner

Isopropyl
alcohol

Abrasive paper

Washing-up
liquid

Cotton buds

White spirit

# Safety equipment

Many DIY activities generate dust, debris, fumes, noise and heat. Buy a personal protective equipment (PPE) kit. These are available from DIY outlets and include safety goggles, a dust mask, ear defenders and gloves.

## Ladders and steps

Falls from access equipment cause more deaths and injuries in the home than any other DIY activity. To avoid them, always set ladders up at the correct angle, with the base of the ladder 1m away from the wall for every 4m of ladder height. If possible, tie the top of the ladder to the building, and ensure that its foot is resting on solid ground or on a level and secure board. Make sure that stepladders are standing square and level.

Don't climb a ladder with your hands full; haul up what you need afterwards using a rope or bucket, or get someone to pass things to you through a nearby window. Don't lean out too far; you or the ladder may slip and fall. Keep your hips within the line of the ladder sides (the stiles), with both feet on the rungs at all times, and hold on to the ladder with one hand whenever possible.

**Ear defenders** Use ear plugs or defenders made to British Standard BS EN 352-4:2001 to protect your hearing during noisy jobs such as drilling masonry.

**A disposable face mask** A simple mask will stop you from inhaling the coarse, airborne, non-toxic dust caused by many drilling, sawing and sanding jobs. If you are spraying paint or creating toxic dust, you should wear a specialist mask made to British Standard BS EN 140:1999.

**Safety goggles** Spectacles or goggles made to British Standard BS EN 166:2002 will protect you from eye injuries whenever you are drilling, sawing, sanding, driving masonry nails or using chemicals, especially above head height. Most safety spectacles and goggles are designed to be large enough to wear comfortably over conventional spectacles.

**Gloves** Always protect your hands when handling coarse building materials or working with chemicals that could harm your skin. Use leather gloves for building work; PVC ones when handling chemicals. Disposable latex gloves can provide useful light-weight protection for many dirty but not potentially harmful jobs.

# Safety in the home

Many accidents in the home are caused by carelessness or a lack of common sense, and could be easily avoided. Follow this advice to escape the most common safety hazards.

## Electrical safety

Electricity can kill. Follow these ten safety precautions to keep yourself safe.

⚠ **Always unplug appliances from the mains** before attempting any repairs and warn others not to reconnect them.

⚠ **Isolate mains circuits at the consumer unit** (see page 22) by switching off miniature circuit breakers (MCBs) or removing circuit fuses before carrying out any work on the house wiring. Make sure others in the house know not to turn them back on while you are working.

⚠ **Uncoil extension leads fully** If the lead is powering any appliance with a heating element, check that the flex rating is suitable for the wattage.

⚠ **Do not overload socket outlets** either with adaptors or by plugging in too many high-wattage appliances. If using a four or six-way adaptor, refer to its back label for the maximum wattage.

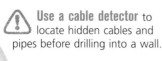

⚠ **Use a cable detector** to locate hidden cables and pipes before drilling into a wall.

⚠ **Keep water and electricity apart** Never plug in appliances or operate switches with wet hands. Never take an electrical appliance into the bathroom or use electrical equipment outside in wet conditions.

⚠ **Check appliance plugs and flexes** regularly for damage, cuts or other signs of wear. Replace damaged parts at the earliest opportunity.

⚠ **Replace blown circuit fuses** using fuse wire or cartridge fuses of the correct rating. Never use any other metallic object to repair a fuse.

---

## HIGH INTERNAL VOLTAGES

Some electronic appliances such as microwaves, televisions, amplifiers and video equipment may retain high internal voltages. Pay attention to any safety warnings on the casing. If in any doubt, do not open the case; contact a qualified repairer.

⚠ **Check that there are earth connections** for all appliances and wiring accessories, and earth all metal pipework and plumbing fittings. You do not need an earth connection in the flex to a non-metallic lampholder or to portable appliances that are double-insulated.

⚠ **Out of doors plug** any power tool being used into a residual current device (RCD) adaptor.

---

## ELECTRIC SHOCK

If somebody receives an electric shock, immediate action is vital.

**1** Do not touch the victim. Turn off the source of the current as quickly as possible. If you cannot do this, grab clothing (not bare flesh, or you will get a shock too) and drag the victim away. Use a wooden broom handle to move them if this is not possible.

**2** If the victim is conscious lay him flat on his back with his legs raised and cover him with a blanket. Turn the head to one side to keep the airway clear and call an ambulance. Soak burns with cold water and cover them with a clean sterile dressing.

**3** If the victim is breathing but unconscious, place him in the recovery position (below). Keep the airway clear by tilting the head back and opening the mouth. Cover him with a blanket and call an ambulance immediately.

## Gas safety

Mains gas will not poison you, but it can explode if it leaks and is ignited. It can also kill indirectly if it is not burned safely and under controlled conditions in a gas fire, boiler or water heater. Always follow these safety guidelines.

**Never attempt DIY work** on your gas pipes, fittings or appliances: this is illegal. Always call in a CORGI-registered fitter to do the work. See page 124 for contact details.

**If you smell a leak** turn off the supply at the main on/off lever (next to the gas meter) – see above. Open all doors and windows. Put out all naked lights and extinguish cigarettes with water. Do not turn any electrical switches either on or off as this can create a spark.

Contact the Transco gas emergency number immediately (0800 111 999) if the smell of gas persists, and call a qualified gas fitter to trace the fault if it disperses.

**Buy only gas appliances** that comply with British or European standards.

**Have gas appliances serviced** at least once a year by a qualified CORGI-registered fitter. Look out for danger signs. If there is soot round an appliance, if it burns with an orange or lazy flame, or if there is excessive condensation nearby, it may be faulty. Call the Transco gas emergency number (above) and stop using it until it has been checked.

**Ensure that rooms** containing gas-burning appliances are properly ventilated. If you get headaches or nausea when they are operating, they may be burning fuel unsafely and creating potentially lethal carbon monoxide (CO) gas. Ask your gas supplier for advice if you are concerned.

**For complete safety**, install a carbon monoxide detector (see box, above right). This is essential if you have gas heaters in bedrooms and regularly use gas or wood burning appliances when you or your family are asleep.

## CARBON MONOXIDE (CO) DETECTORS

A carbon monoxide detector is not the same as a smoke detector. It detects dangerous, odourless and invisible CO gas, which can be produced by faulty fuel-burning appliances. Buy a CO detector made to British Standard BS7860.

Detectors must be placed 1.5m above floor level (CO is lighter than air, and rises to the ceiling) and around 2m from an appliance. Push the test button once a month to check the battery and replace the batteries annually. Replace the whole detector unit after five years (although some models are guaranteed for ten years).

## Fire

Be alert to the dangers of fire. A fire can be caused by an electrical fault, by careless use of tools that generate heat, such as a blowlamp, or by careless use or storage of flammable materials. Keep a fire blanket in the kitchen and an all-purpose fire extinguisher in the garage for emergencies.

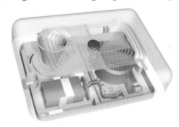

Smoke detectors must now be fitted, by law, in all new houses. If your house does not have any, it is wise to fit them straight away. Detectors should be fitted within 7.5m of the doorway to every habitable room in the house. They should be fixed to the ceiling, 30cm or more from any wall. Make sure all smoke detectors are made to British Standard BS 5446-1:2000.

Test each alarm at least once a month to check that the battery is not flat on battery-powered models. Vacuum the detector inside and out at the same time. If your detector emits a regular beep, it is a sign that the battery is low. Replace the battery annually even if it still has life in it – unless your model runs on a ten-year lithium cell.

A heat detector is a good alternative in a kitchen, where a smoke detector may be activated by cooking fumes.

# Around the house

# The electrical system

**Before you do any electrical work you should get to grips with the different types of circuit in your home.**

Electric power is measured in **watts** (W). The flow of electricity is called current, and is measured in **amps** (A). The driving force, or pressure, of the current is measured in **volts** (V), standardised at 230 volts in Britain. Mains electricity is **alternating current** (AC); this can be transformed from one voltage to another so a power station can supply a very high voltage to local substations, which reduce the voltage to 230V to supply homes.

**Lighting circuit** The circuit runs out from the consumer unit, linking a chain of lighting points. Cables run from each lighting point to its switch. The circuit is protected by a 5 or 6amp circuit fuse or MCB. It can safely supply up to a maximum of about 1200 watts, but in practice should not serve more than ten lighting points. The circuit would be overloaded if each of the lighting points had high-wattage bulbs.

**Ring main circuit** The circuit is wired as a ring that starts at the consumer unit and returns to it, allowing current to flow to socket outlets either way round the ring. It can serve a floor area of up to 100m². It is protected by a 30 or 32amp circuit fuse or MCB. It can have any number of sockets or fused connection units on it, but its maximum total load is about 7000 watts. For larger total loads and larger floor areas, additional ring circuits are needed.

**Spur on a ring circuit** Extra socket outlets can be added to an existing ring main circuit via spurs branching off the ring at a socket outlet or junction box. In theory, each outlet on the ring could supply a spur to a single or double socket or a fused connection unit. However, the circuit including any spurs must not serve rooms with a floor area of more than 100m² – and its maximum load is still 7000 watts.

**Socket outlet** The maximum load that can be supplied by a socket outlet is 3000 watts. The plug is fitted with a 3amp or 13amp fuse, according to the wattage rating of the appliance connected to it.

**Single-appliance circuit** An appliance that is a heavy consumer of electricity and is in constant or frequent use – a cooker, fixed water heater or shower heater unit, for example – has its own circuit running from the consumer unit. It would be likely to overload a shared circuit.

**The consumer unit** The consumer unit contains labelled trip switches called MCBs (miniature circuit breakers) for all the circuits in your home. This allows you to isolate a circuit so that you can work on it in safety. Older consumer units (fuse boxes) are fitted with either rewirable or replaceable fuses.

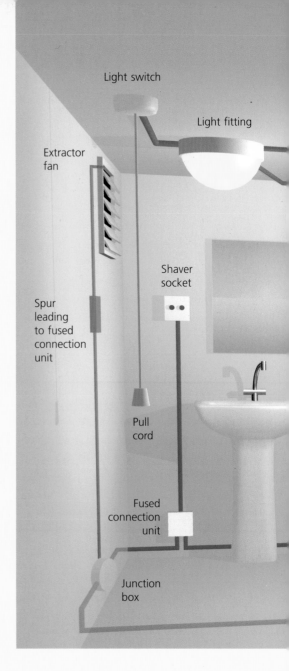

Light switch

Light fitting

Extractor fan

Shaver socket

Spur leading to fused connection unit

Pull cord

Fused connection unit

Junction box

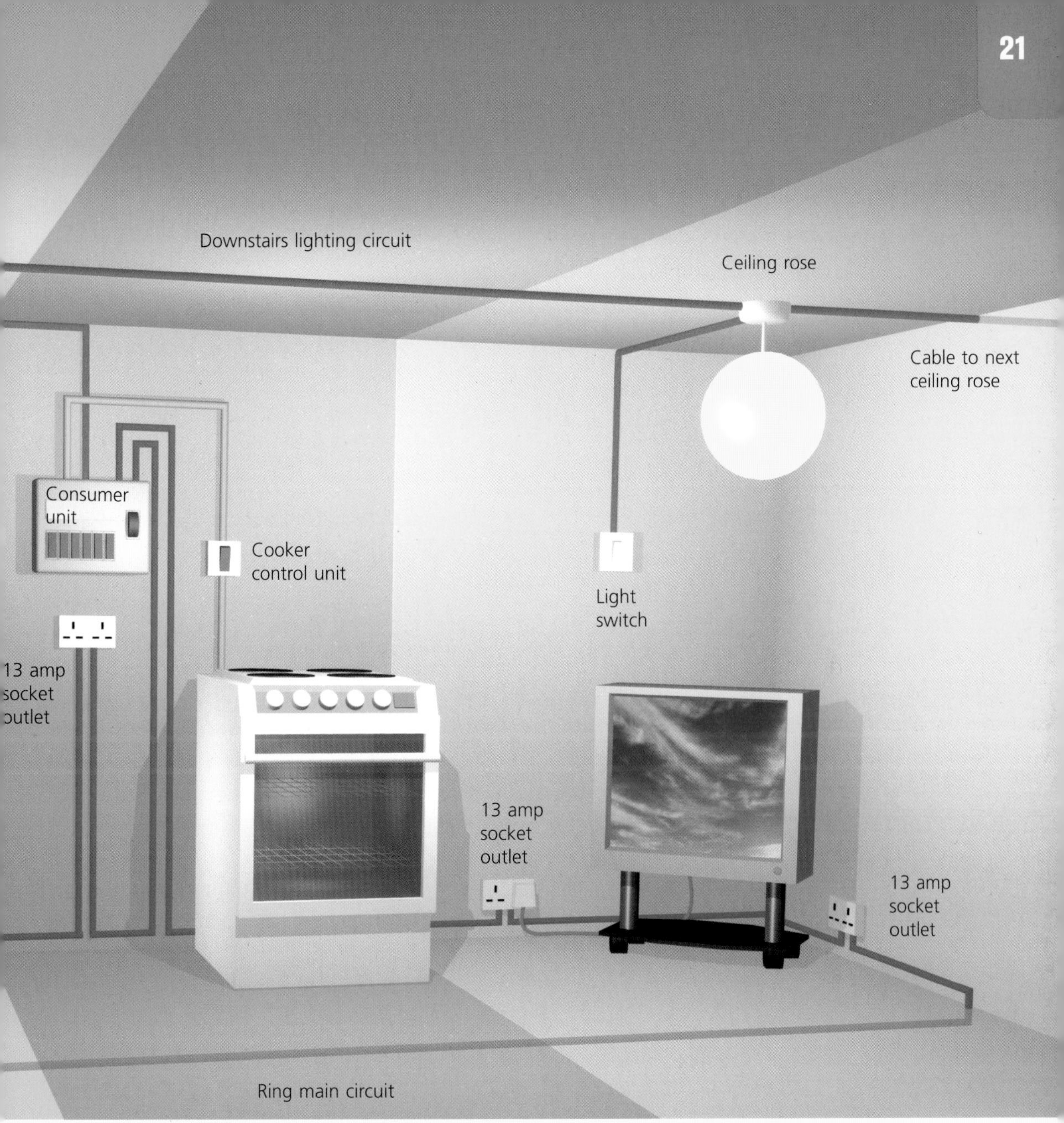

Downstairs lighting circuit

Ceiling rose

Cable to next
ceiling rose

Consumer
unit

Cooker
control unit

Light
switch

13 amp
socket
outlet

13 amp
socket
outlet

13 amp
socket
outlet

Ring main circuit

## SAFETY WARNING

All new electrical installation work must satisfy Part P of the Building
Regulations. Homeowners must be able to prove that new fixed installations and alterations have been inspected and tested by a competent
electrician. Most wiring jobs, including all new work in a kitchen or
bathroom, must be notified to your local Building Control inspector or
be carried out by an electrician who can issue the necessary certificates.

Minor jobs, such as adding new lights or socket outlets to existing
circuits (except in kitchens and bathrooms) and replacing existing
accessories do not need to be notified, though they must still be checked
and certified. If you are unsure, check with your local Building Control
department and always leave electrical work to a qualified electrician,
unless you are confident you can carry it out safely and correctly.

# The consumer unit

Modern fuse boards – called consumer units – may look different from home to home, but the basic components are the same.

**Consumer unit** The householder's responsibility for the system begins here. It houses the main on-off switch, the earthing terminal block for all the house circuits, and individual fuses or miniature circuit breakers (MCBs) for each one.
• The number of circuits varies according to a household's needs, but always includes separate lighting and power circuits.
• Label the MCBs to show which circuit each one protects. To identify the circuits, switch off one MCB at a time and check which lights or appliances are not working.

**Service cable** Electricity enters the home through the service (supply) cable, usually buried underground in urban areas, but often run overhead in rural areas. It carries electricity at 230 volts. Never interfere with the service cable: it is the property of your electricity provider.

**Sealed unit/service cut-out** The service cable ends here. The unit contains a fuse (the service cut-out), usually rated at 60amps or, in modern installations, 100amps. It is a deliberate weak link that will melt and disconnect the supply to the house if more current is demanded than the service cable can safely supply. **Do not tamper with the sealed unit.**

**Miniature circuit breakers (MCBs)**
Modern consumer units have MCBs instead of fuses. If too much current is demanded, the circuit is disconnected instantly and a switch moves to the 'off' position or a button pops out. Reset the switch to restore power to the circuit.

---

## MCB CURRENT RATINGS

As part of a move towards European standardisation, the ratings marked on new MCBs have been changed.

| | |
|---|---|
| 5amp is now | 6 amp |
| 15amp is now | 16amp |
| 30amp is now | 32amp |
| 45amp is now | 40amp or 50amp |

---

In older systems, each circuit is protected by a fuse, not an MCB. These fuseholders (below) have slot-in rewirable fuse carriers or sealed cartridges. Each is marked with the amp rating of the fuse if contains. A lighting circuit is protected by a 5A fuse, and a ring main circuit by a 30A fuse.

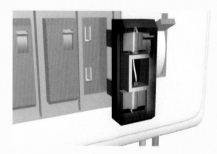

Within each of the fuse carriers or cartridges is a length of fuse wire. If the current demanded by the circuit exceeds the rating, the fuse wire melts ('blows') and the circuit is disconnected. Always keep a supply of replacement wires or cartridges in a range of appropriate amp ratings.

**Residual current device (RCD)**
An RCD monitors the balance of the live and neutral current flows. An imbalance occurs if current leaks from a circuit because of faulty insulation, or because

---

## MAINTENANCE

### ONCE EVERY THREE MONTHS

Test RCD in consumer unit *Make sure all major appliances are turned off and that everyone else in the house knows the power is to be cut temporarily. Push RCD test button (see left). Switch should flip to the off position. If nothing happens, contact electrician immediately. If switch trips correctly, reset switch to the on position to reconnect power.*

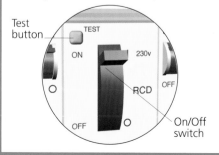

Test button

On/Off switch

someone has touched a live part and received an electric shock. If the RCD detects an imbalance, it switches off the supply immediately – fast enough to prevent an electric shock from being fatal.

• When RCDs were first introduced, they often replaced the system's main on-off switch. This practice has now been discontinued because it was found unnecessary for all circuits to be RCD-protected. An RCD is now installed to protect only at-risk circuits such as those to socket outlets and some stand-alone appliances.

• An RCD in its own enclosure may have been added to an existing installation to protect new at-risk circuits.

**Circuit cables** Individual circuits are supplied by cables running out from the consumer unit. The live conductor in each circuit cable is connected to a terminal on its fuse or MCB. The neutral conductor connects to the main neutral terminal block in the consumer unit, and the earth to the main earthing terminal block.

**Earthing cable** This connects the earthing terminal block in the consumer unit to the earthing point provided by the electricity supply company – usually on the service cut-out or the service cable. Earth cross-bonding cables connect metal pipework to the earthing terminal block.

**Meter** A two-tariff meter with two displays may be installed to allow the use of night-rate electricity for storage heaters.

**Meter tails** These two cables (live and neutral) link the sealed unit to the meter and the meter to the consumer unit.

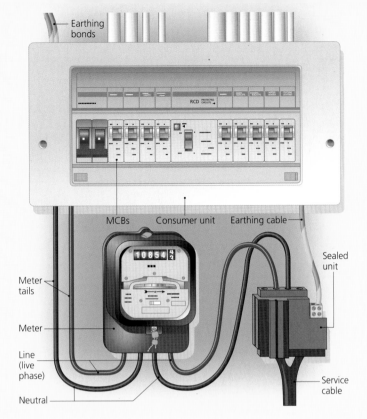

Earthing bonds

MCBs    Consumer unit    Earthing cable

Meter tails

Meter

Line (live phase)

Neutral

Sealed unit

Service cable

---

## FAULT DIAGNOSIS

### MILD SHOCK FROM METAL-CASED DEVICE

Earth fault within item *Contact a qualified repairer. This fault should have tripped an RCD, so test yours, or have one fitted if none is present.*

### NO POWER

MCB tripped *Turn off appliances, reset switch. Unplug all appliances, then reconnect them one by one to identify faulty device. If an appliance repeatedly causes its MCB to trip, stop using it, unplug it and have it checked.*
Whole house RCD tripped *Reset RCD. If fault recurs, call qualified electrician.*
Local power failure *Check adjacent buildings to verify, and report power failure to your electricity company.*
Service fuse blown *Call electricity company immediately to replace.*

### MCB TRIPS REGULARLY

Circuit overload *Caused by plugging in too many high-wattage appliances at once. Maximum for a circuit is 7kW.*

# Fitting a new plug

New appliances are sold with factory-fitted plugs – you only need to change the fuse if the original blows. But if you need to replace a damaged plug, it is essential to do it correctly.

The three pins of a plug are connected to the live, neutral and earth conductors in the flex. The earth pin is longer than the others, so that the earth contact is made first as the plug is pushed into the socket outlet. On new plugs the live and neutral pins are partly insulated to prevent fingers coming into contact with the metal pins as the plug is inserted or withdrawn.

To get power to the appliance the current must pass through the fuse, which sits between the live pin and the live flex terminal. The fuse contains a fine strip of metal. If the current drawn from the mains is too large the fuse wire will overheat and melt, stopping the excessive current from damaging the appliance.

All three-pin plugs are fitted with a cartridge fuse. Many contain a 13amp fuse when you buy them, but you should fit a lower-rated fuse if the appliance rating is below 700 watts.

**Tools** *Insulated screwdrivers; sharp knife; wire cutters and strippers; pliers.*

**Materials** *Plug; flex; cartridge fuse (either 3amp or 13amp).*

**1** Unscrew the cover of the new plug and remove it.

**2** Prise out the cartridge fuse if necessary to reveal the terminal. Loosen the screw-down bar that secures the flex if there is one. Plastic jaws grip the flex in some plugs.

**3** If you are replacing a hand-wired plug, remove its cover and loosen the terminal screws to release the flex cores from their terminals. Release the flex from the flex grip. Inspect the bare cores. If they appear damaged, cut them off and strip off some core insulation to expose undamaged wires ready for reconnection to the new plug. If you are replacing a factory-fitted plug, cut through the flex close to the plug body.

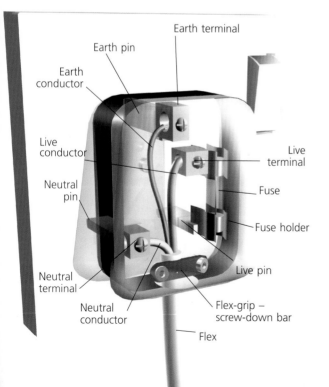

Earth terminal

Earth pin

Earth conductor

Live conductor

Live terminal

Neutral pin

Fuse

Fuse holder

Live pin

Neutral terminal

Neutral conductor

Flex-grip – screw-down bar

Flex

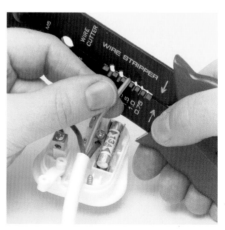

**4** Prepare the end of the cut flex, by stripping away the necessary insulation. For some plugs all the cores have to be the same length, for others they have to be different lengths. Check that the prepared

| SAFETY CHECK | FAULT DIAGNOSIS |
|---|---|
| ONCE EVERY SIX MONTHS | NO POWER TO APPLIANCE |

Check flexes and plugs for damage *This is particularly important with appliances which are portable or which are moved during use, such as a hair dryer, iron, vacuum cleaner or power tool. Replace if necessary.*

Cracked plug/live parts exposed *Replace plug.*
Fuse blown *Unplug appliance and check plug and flex for evidence of scorching caused by a short circuit. Replace flex if necessary. Fit replacement fuse of correct rating and test the appliance.*
MCB tripped or circuit fuse blown *Reset MCB (see page 22) or replace blown fuse. If fault reoccurs contact an electrician.*
Flex discontinuity *Check each conductor with a continuity tester and replace the flex if faulty.*

cores are long enough to reach their terminals with the flex sheath held in the flex grip.

**5** Tough rubber plugs designed for use on power tools have a hole in the plug cover through which the flex passes before being connected to the plug terminals.

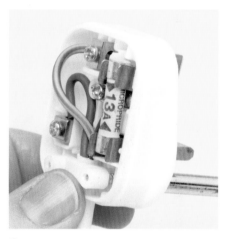

**6** Connect each flex core to its correct terminal. The **BR**own (live) core goes to the **B**ottom **R**ight terminal, the **BL**ue (neutral) core to the **B**ottom **L**eft terminal, and the earth core in three-core flex (green-and-yellow) to the top terminal.

**7** With pillar-type terminals, loosen the terminal screw and insert the bare end of the core in the hole. Tighten the screw to trap it in place. Plugs with this type of terminal often have loose pins; remove these from the plug first if it makes connecting the cores easier.

**Alternatively** With screw-down stud terminals, remove the stud and wind the bare end of the core clockwise round the threaded peg. Screw the stud down to trap the wires in place.

**8** Arrange the cores in their channels in the plug body and place the flex sheath in the cord grip. If the plug has nylon jaws, press the flex in between them. If it has a screw-down bar, undo one screw, position the flex in the grip, swing the bar back over it and screw it down securely. Fit the fuse.

**9** Replace the plug cover and make sure that it is firmly screwed together.

# Socket outlets

Most electrical appliances can be plugged in at any socket outlet, which may be sunk into the wall or surface mounted. Fixed appliances, such as cooker hoods, are connected directly to the power circuit using fused connection units (FCUs), which are protected by a dedicated fuse.

As a plug is inserted into a socket outlet, the earth pin enters first because it is longest. Its pushes open the protective shutters from in front of the live and neutral pin holes.

When a plug is fully inserted, all three pins make contact with their corresponding sprung connectors inside the socket outlet. These are connected to the wiring terminals. When the socket switch is moved

## CABLE COLOUR CHANGE

The colours shown here reflect what you will see on existing household wiring. However, use of cables with new colours is now compulsory for all new wiring in the home. In two-core-and-earth cable, the red core will change to brown and the black core to blue, making them identical to the colours used on flex cores. Where new cable is wired into an exisiting fitting, you will see both old and new together.

to the on position, the contacts complete a circuit by linking the live terminal to the live sprung connector. Power flows from the ring main via the live pin through the flex to the appliance. The circuit is completed via the neutral pin. A flying earth link ensures the metal box is earthed.

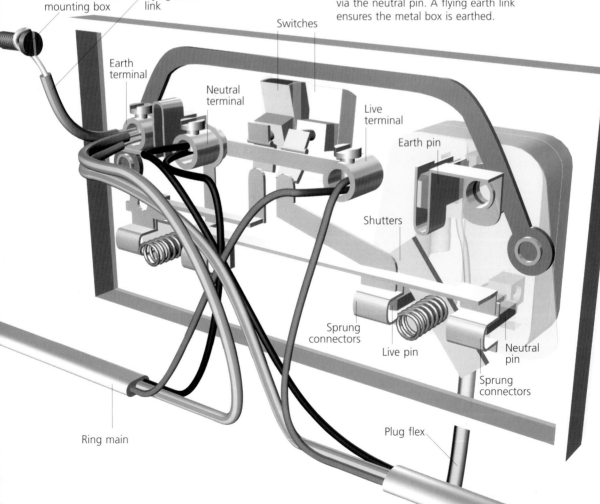

Earth terminal in mounting box

Flying earth link

Switches

Earth terminal

Neutral terminal

Live terminal

Earth pin

Shutters

Sprung connectors

Live pin

Neutral pin

Sprung connectors

Ring main

Plug flex

MAINTENANCE

## MAINTENANCE

### ONCE A YEAR

Test socket outlets using a socket tester *This is an inexpensive device that plugs into each socket outlet and warns of wiring problems (see below).*

## FAULT DIAGNOSIS

### SOCKET OUTLET NOT WORKING

Worn or damaged outlet
*Replace socket outlet.*
Cable disconnected inside outlet
*Turn off mains and check that connections to terminals are secure.*
Dirt in connectors or switch
*Replace socket outlet.*
MCB tripped *Trace and rectify fault. Replace fuse or switch MCB back on (see Consumer unit, page 22).*

## Testing the socket outlets

Use a mains tester unit to check each socket outlet in turn. Up to three lights will come on in different combinations to indicate that the socket is correctly wired or that it has a fault. Check the chart on the body of the tester (or the tester manufacturer's instructions) to identify specific faults.

## Replacing a socket outlet

**1** Turn off the main power switch and also remove the fuse or turn off the miniature circuit breaker (MCB) (see Consumer unit, page 22) for the circuit on which you are working. Switch the power back on to the other circuits. Test the socket outlet with a lamp to make sure the power is off. Undo the screws holding the faceplate in place and pull it away from the mounting box.

**2** A socket outlet on a ring main has two cores in each terminal. If there is one core in each terminal, the outlet is a spur (ie it is wired to a socket that is itself on the ring main). If there are three, it supplies a spur. Connect the new outlet in exactly the same way as the old one – red to live, black to neutral and green/yellow to earth. Reconnect the earth link between the faceplate and mounting box, as shown.

**3** Make sure that none of the wires will be twisted or caught as you fold them back into the box. If the earth link is missing, use the earth wire from a cable offcut to create an earth link. If earth wires are bare, cover them with a green/yellow sleeving. Screw the faceplate back on and then replace the fuse or reset the MCB and switch the power on. Test the socket with a mains tester (above left) before use.

# Replacing lights and switches

All the light fittings in a circuit are connected in a chain, with switch cables connected into each lighting point. There are usually separate circuits for upstairs and downstairs.

Lighting cable is twin-core-and-earth, with live, neutral and earth cores. The bare earth cores are covered in slip-on green-and yellow PVC sleeving when exposed. This cable carries the power for all the lights on the circuit. The flex to each lampholder is of a lower rating and only needs an earth core if the lampholder is metal.

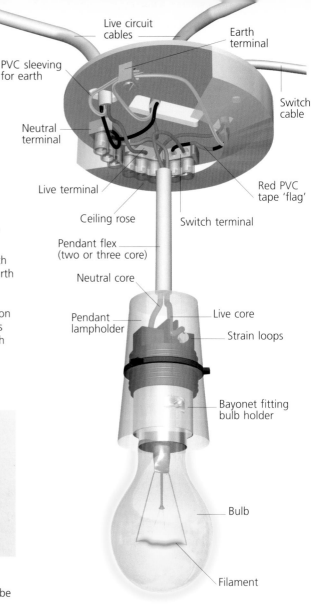

Live circuit cables

Earth terminal

PVC sleeving for earth

Switch cable

Neutral terminal

Red PVC tape 'flag'

Live terminal

Ceiling rose

Switch terminal

Pendant flex (two or three core)

Neutral core

Live core

Pendant lampholder

Strain loops

Bayonet fitting bulb holder

Bulb

Filament

## Replacing a switch

**1** Turn off the power at the mains and unscrew the switch faceplate. There will be a red and a black core connected to the switch. There should be a flag of red PVC insulating tape on the black core at the switch and at the light fitting. This indicates that the black core (the colour normally used for neutral) is live when the switch is on. The earth core is connected to the earth terminal in the mounting box. Undo the retaining screws in the terminals and release the cores to remove the switch.

**2** Reconnect the cores as before. In a 2-way switch used for 1-way switching, connect the red core to 'common' and black (flagged with red PVC insulating tape) to 'L1' or 'L2'. If the switch is metal, fit a short length of earth core (with green and yellow PVC sleeving) to link the earth terminals on the faceplate and metal mounting box to the earth.

### SAFETY WARNING

Before starting work on a light switch or fitting, turn the power off at the consumer unit and remove the fuseholder or switch off the MCB protecting the circuit you are working on. Switch other circuits back on. Turning off the light at the wall switch does not make the fitting safe to work on.

## FAULT DIAGNOSIS

### SPARKING LIGHT SWITCH

Worn or dirty contacts *Replace switch.*

### BROKEN CEILING ROSE COVER

Impact damage *Replace rose. If in any doubt about correct wiring, contact qualified electrician.*

### BROKEN OR BRITTLE LAMPHOLDER

Impact damage or heat from lamp *Replace lampholder.*

### CRACKED SWITCH FACEPLATE

Impact damage *Replace switch.*

## Replacing a recessed bulb

**1** Gently squeeze together the two ends of the metal circlip that should be just visible around the inner edge of the fitting. Remove the circlip and the bulb will be released from its housing and will dangle out of the hole in the ceiling.

**2** The bulb is attached to the cable by a plug with two pins on it. Carefully pull the plug away from the bulb, then connect it to the new bulb. Push the bulb back up into the ceiling recess and replace the circlip to hold it in place.

## Replacing a lampholder

**1** Turn off the power for the lighting circuit and test the light to make sure the power is off. Remove the bulb and unscrew the shade ring. Remove the shade and unscrew the top cover.

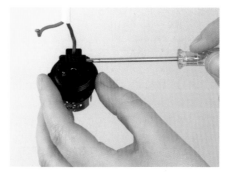

**2** Using an electrician's screwdriver, unclip the flex cores from the strain loops at the top of the fitting and disconnect from the terminals. Remove the lampholder and the cover from the flex.

**3** Slide the new cover on to the flex and attach the flex cores to the terminals. Hook the cores over the strain loops and screw on the upper cover. Refit the shade, shade ring and bulb and restore the power to the circuit.

# How water is supplied to the home

Whether for home improvements, or for tackling emergencies, it is important to know what type of water system you have, and where to find all the relevant system controls.

## WATER METERS

If your house has a water meter, it will be installed outside the property boundary, between the water main and the outdoor stoptap.

# Getting water into your home

The water supply to most British homes is provided by the local water supply company, through iron or heavy plastic water mains. From here, a pipe known as a communication pipe takes the water to the water company's stoptap, a control valve about 1m below ground at or near the boundary of each property. This is where the householder's responsibility for the pipework begins, and in older properties it may be the only place where the water can be turned off.

Water is carried into the house via the service pipe, which usually enters the house close to the kitchen sink (but sometimes under the stairs or in a garage). An indoor stoptap should be fitted here for cutting off the house water supply. From here, the rising main, a 15mm diameter pipe, feeds the household supply.

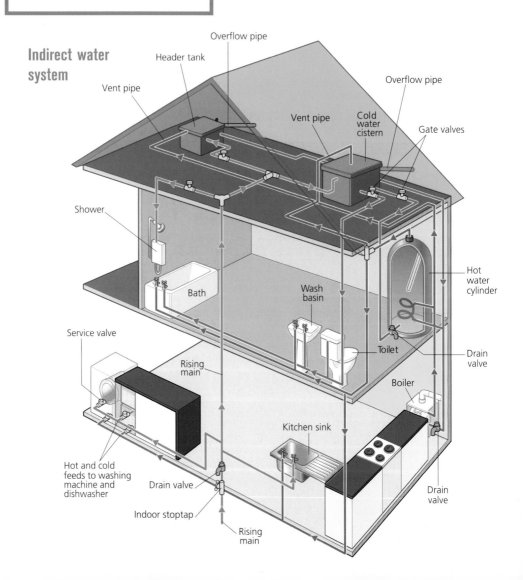

**Indirect water system**

Overflow pipe

Header tank

Vent pipe

Vent pipe

Cold water cistern

Overflow pipe

Gate valves

Shower

Hot water cylinder

Bath

Wash basin

Toilet

Drain valve

Service valve

Rising main

Boiler

Hot and cold feeds to washing machine and dishwasher

Drain valve

Kitchen sink

Indoor stoptap

Rising main

Drain valve

## TURNING OFF THE SUPPLY

The outdoor stoptap, which is turned with a long key, is under a metal cover in the front garden or the pavement outside.

# The cold water supply

There are two types of cold water supply in British homes: direct and indirect.

A direct system In a direct cold water supply, branch pipes from the rising main lead directly to all the cold taps and WC cisterns in the house. This means that you can drink cold water from any tap. A pipe from the rising main will usually feed a storage cistern in the loft that feeds the hot water cylinder. A direct cold water system is simpler and cheaper to install than an indirect system.

An indirect system Most British homes have an indirect system (left). The rising main feeds the cold tap at the kitchen sink (and possibly a washing machine, outside tap or electric shower). This is drinking water. It then continues up to a storage tank in the roof, which supplies all other taps, the WCs and the hot water cylinder.
  The level of the water in the cold water storage tank is maintained by a float valve, or ballvalve. As the level drops the float lowers, opening an inlet valve. As soon as the water – and the float – rises to the correct level, the valve is closed.
  There are advantages to an indirect system: water from a storage tank gives even water pressure, which produces quieter plumbing and less wear and tear on washers and valves. Leaks are also less likely, and will be less damaging than one from a pipe under mains pressure.
  Cold water from a cistern is warmer than mains water, so less hot water is needed for washing and bathing. It also reduces condensation on WC cisterns. And if the house supply is temporarily cut off – for work on the mains, for example – there is a supply of stored water available for use.

## SAFETY NOTE

If your house has an indirect system, do not drink water from any tap other than the kitchen one. Water from a tank may not be clean.

# The hot water supply

There are also two basic hot water systems: indirect, with all hot taps supplied from a hot water storage cylinder, or direct, where cold water is heated on demand. The latter is usual when the cold water supply is also through a direct system.
  Back boilers and separate kitchen boilers have largely been replaced by modern boilers that supply both hot water and central heating.

## Indirect hot-water systems

You can identify an indirect system by the two water tanks in the loft (see diagram opposite). The second, smaller tank is called a header tank, or feed and expansion tank; it keeps the primary circuit topped up. The level of water in the header tank is low enough to allow the water to expand when it gets hot without overflowing.

The primary circuit With an indirect water system, the hot water cylinder contains a coil of pipe, which forms part of a run of pipework connected to the boiler. This is heated directly by the boiler. Indirectly, it heats the water in the cylinder. The coil, or heat exchanger, is actually part of the central heating circuit: its water heating function arises out of its main job, which is to heat the radiators. This heating pipework is known as the 'primary' circuit and the pipes that run to and from the boiler are known as the primary flow and return.

The secondary circuit Water in the hot water cylinder is supplied from the cold water cistern, which keeps the cylinder constantly topped up as hot water is used. A vent pipe from the top of the hot water cylinder hangs over the cold water cistern, allowing air to escape. Pipes to the hot taps lead from the vent pipe. Because these branch pipes leave above the cylinder top, the cylinder cannot be drained through the hot taps. This means you don't need to turn off the boiler if the household water supply is temporarily cut off.
  This system is known as a vented system. It is open to atmospheric pressure and operates under low pressure. A pump can be fitted to boost flow to showers or taps.

**Unvented (sealed) hot water systems**
This system is the same as an indirect system, except that it is connected to the mains. This gives mains water pressure to hot taps and showers. Many safety features are built into this type of system to allow for the greater pressure and expansion of the water. No cold water storage cistern or header tank is needed, so there is no pipework in the loft.

## Direct hot water systems

In older houses with a direct system (often back boilers or solid-fuel boilers), the water is heated directly by circulation through the boiler. Water is fed from the cold water cistern into the bottom of the cylinder and then to the boiler. The flow pipe from the top of the boiler discharges hot water directly into the top of the cylinder, forcing colder, denser water at the bottom through the return pipe back to the boiler. The hottest water, being the lightest, is always at the top ready to be drawn off.

**Immersion heater** This is another form of direct heating (see page 58). The hot water cylinder can be heated by one or two electric immersion heaters. About 1kW of heat is needed for every 45 litres of water, so a 140-litre hot water cylinder needs a 3kW heater. Today, an immersion heater is rarely the sole form of water heating in the home. Rather, it is used to supplement a boiler system or as a way to heat water in summer when the central heating boiler is switched off.

An immersion heater has a thermostat to control the water temperature. For most homes, 55–60°C is ideal.

## Insulating pipes

**1** Cut split-sleeve foam insulation with a knife to the correct lengths and trim the ends at a 45° angle at elbows and tees. Use PVC tape to seal the joints.

**2** Where the pipe curves, cut v-shaped notches out of one side of the insulation and bend the insulation round the curve with the cuts on the inside of the bend.

---

### FAULT DIAGNOSIS

#### LEAKING PIPE

Burst or leaking pipe *Turn off water and drain cold water cistern by opening all cold taps. Then repair pipe or call emergency plumber.*

#### NO WATER FROM TAPS

No supply from rising main *Check main stoptap is open. If it is, contact water supply company. You can find the number under 'Water' in the phone book.*
Jammed ballvalve in cistern *Check whether cistern is filling. If not, depress the float arm to free the valve and fill the cistern. If this fails, replace the ballvalve.*

#### OVERFLOW DRIPPING

Faulty ballvalve *Service or replace ballvalve.*
Float arm too high *Adjust float position or bend arm downwards to lower water level in cistern.*

#### FROZEN PIPES

No lagging or temperature dropped too low *Defrost pipes with a hot-water bottle or hair dryer and lag with split-sleeve foam pipe insulation.*

## Replacing a float valve

**1** Turn off the main indoor stoptap. Use an adjustable spanner to undo the tap connector attaching the supply pipe to the valve at the cold water cistern, and then disconnect the supply pipe. Keep a towel handy to mop up any drips.

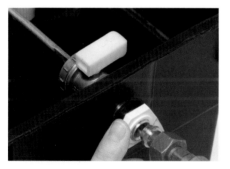

**2** Use the spanner to loosen the back nut holding the valve to the outside of the cistern, then unscrew the nut by hand and remove the valve. Remove the back nut from the new valve and put it to one side.

**3** Put a new flat plastic washer over the valve tail (and an inner locking nut if supplied) and fit the new valve to the cistern, making sure it is orientated correctly (in the same position as before).

**4** Put another plastic washer over the outside of the valve tail and screw on the back nut by hand, before tightening it half a turn with the adjustable spanner. Disconnect the existing tap connector and in its place fit a service valve that has a tap connector at one end and a 15mm compression fitting at the other. Use a screwdriver to open the service valve fully and then turn the water back on at the main indoor stoptap.

**5** Check the water level of the cistern when the valve shuts – it should be 25mm below the level of the overflow. Adjust the water level if necessary by loosening the float nut and sliding the float up or down the arm. Slide it up to raise the water level or down to lower it, and then tighten the float nut. On older, piston-type valves, the only way to adjust the float height is to bend the arm.

### DEFROSTING PIPES

First check that the pipe has not burst and have towels and bowls to hand in case of leaks. Locate the frozen section of pipe by checking which taps have stopped working. Then turn off the indoor stoptap. Remove any insulation from the frozen pipe and open the nearest tap to allow water to escape as it expands. Wrap a hot water bottle around the pipe, or use a hair dryer to heat the pipe. Never use a heat gun or blowlamp to defrost a pipe.

Replace the insulation or fit some if none was present before. Close the tap then open the main stoptap and check for split pipes or parted joints.

# Taps

All taps work in more or less the same way – a rotating handle opens and closes a valve, allowing water to flow through. Drips and leaks are the most common problems, as seals and washers become worn.

Traditional taps use a system of nuts and screws to open a valve. In others, one ceramic disc is rotated against another until their openings line up. Their problems and the solutions differ from design to design.

## Shrouded head rising spindle tap

When the tap is closed, a washer is held over the hole in the seat by a jumper. As the capstan head is turned anti-clockwise, the spindle rises, lifting the washer away from the seat and allowing water through.

The spindle screws up and down within a gland nut, which is filled with watertight packing to prevent water leaking up past the spindle when the tap is turned on. In time, the washer can perish, causing the tap to drip, or the packing can fail, causing a leak from the body of the tap.

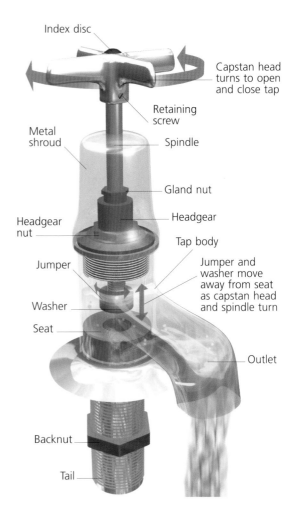

Index disc

Capstan head turns to open and close tap

Retaining screw

Metal shroud

Spindle

Gland nut

Headgear nut

Headgear

Tap body

Jumper

Jumper and washer move away from seat as capstan head and spindle turn

Washer

Seat

Outlet

Backnut

Tail

## Rising spindle tap: curing a leaking spindle

**1** Lever off the index disc and unscrew the retaining screw and the tap's handle. Use a wrench wrapped in cloth to unscrew the metal shroud. Grip the headgear nut with a spanner then use another spanner to tighten the gland nut by half a turn. Slip the handle back on and check the tap. If it still leaks, tighten the gland nut by another half turn and check again.

**2** If the spindle still leaks, remove the gland nut completely and lift it out. Make a note of the packing used – it could be string, hemp, graphite or a rubber O-ring. Replace string packing with fibre string or PTFE tape, and reassemble the tap.

## MAINTENANCE

### ONCE A YEAR

Check taps for hard water damage *If you live in a hard water area, turn off mains supply and supply from the tank (usually found in the airing cupboard or loft). Check headgear on each tap unscrews easily. Use penetrating oil to release stiff nuts and use spanner and wrench wrapped in cloth to hold body of tap to avoid scratching it with metal tools. Soak parts in vinegar or limescale remover if limescale is present. Smear thread and washer with silicone lubricant before reassembling.*

**Before you start the job**
While working on taps, it is a good idea to put the plug in the plughole to stop small parts being lost. Protect the sink or bath with a towel so that you do not scratch or chip the enamel or chinaware with accidentally dropped tools.

## Rising spindle tap: replacing a washer

Remove the small screw beneath the index disc to release the capstan from the spindle. Use a wrench wrapped in cloth to unscrew the metal shroud and lift it away from the headgear nut. Then, follow the steps for replacing a worn washer in a non-rising spindle tap (see page 37).

## FAULT DIAGNOSIS

*Fault diagnosis and repair will vary depending on type of tap.*

### DRIPPING TAP

Non-rising spindle tap: worn washer *Replace washer.*
Ceramic disc tap: worn rubber seal *Replace.*
Ceramic disc tap: faulty cartridge *Clean inside or replace cartridge.*
Rising spindle tap: worn washer *Replace washer.*
Traditional tap: damaged valve seat *Cover seat with nylon liner, sold by plumbing suppliers with matching jumper and washer. Follow manufacturer's instructions.*

### LEAKING SPINDLE

Non-rising spindle tap: worn O-ring *Replace.*
Rising spindle tap: loose gland nut or gland packing faulty *Tighten nut and check packing.*
Mixer tap: worn O-ring on spout *Replace.*

### TAP 'SCREAMS' WHEN OPEN

Worn jumper *Replace washer and jumper assembly.*
Rising spindle tap only: loose spindle *Tighten gland nut.*

### TAP THUDS AND BANGS WHEN OFF

Loose washer *This can flutter in water stream, sending shockwaves (water hammer) through system. Replace washer. If problem persists, install water hammer arrestor.*
Worn or cracked ceramic discs *Replace cartridge.*

### TAP STUCK OR DIFFICULT TO OPEN

Hard water damage *Dismantle and clean (see maintenance).*
Worn or cracked ceramic discs *Replace cartridge.*

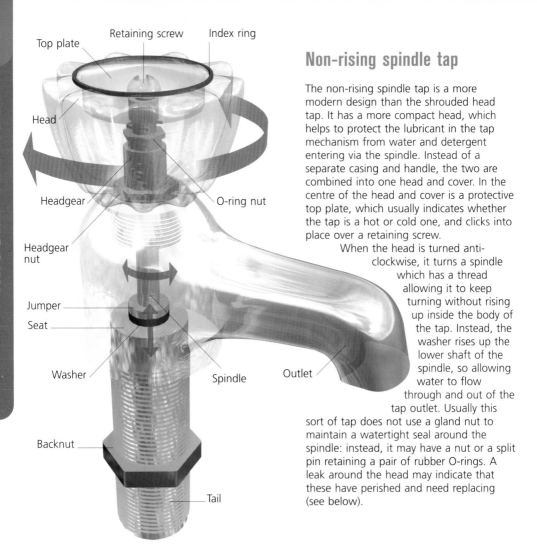

Top plate
Retaining screw
Index ring
Head
Headgear
O-ring nut
Headgear nut
Jumper
Seat
Washer
Spindle
Outlet
Backnut
Tail

## Non-rising spindle tap

The non-rising spindle tap is a more modern design than the shrouded head tap. It has a more compact head, which helps to protect the lubricant in the tap mechanism from water and detergent entering via the spindle. Instead of a separate casing and handle, the two are combined into one head and cover. In the centre of the head and cover is a protective top plate, which usually indicates whether the tap is a hot or cold one, and clicks into place over a retaining screw.

When the head is turned anti-clockwise, it turns a spindle which has a thread allowing it to keep turning without rising up inside the body of the tap. Instead, the washer rises up the lower shaft of the spindle, so allowing water to flow through and out of the tap outlet. Usually this sort of tap does not use a gland nut to maintain a watertight seal around the spindle: instead, it may have a nut or a split pin retaining a pair of rubber O-rings. A leak around the head may indicate that these have perished and need replacing (see below).

## Non-rising spindle tap: replacing O-rings

**1** Follow steps 1–3 opposite to remove the headgear. Turn the spindle clockwise, lever out the circlip (above) or unscrew the nut to release the spindle.

**2** Lever the O-rings from the spindle and fit replacements that are the same size. Smear the spindle with silicone grease before reassembling the tap.

## Non-rising spindle tap: replacing a worn washer

**1** Turn off the water supply, make sure the tap is turned on fully and wait until water stops flowing. Unscrew or lever off the top plate with a screwdriver.

**2** Remove the retaining screw and pull off the head, putting the screw in a safe place.

**3** Use a spanner to undo the headgear nut. Do not force the nut if it is stiff. Brace the tap body by hand or with a pipe wrench wrapped in cloth, to prevent the tap from turning and fracturing the pipework supplying it.

### DEALING WITH A DRIPPING TAP

Always fix dripping taps promptly. A persistent drip is not only a waste of water, but will eventually stain the surface of the bath or basin it is dripping into.

In conventional taps this usually means replacing the washer, although turning over and refitting the old washer may temporarily fix the problem. If a scratched ceramic disc is causing the leak, the entire cartridge must be replaced: left-handed for a hot tap or right-handed for a cold tap. Remove the old cartridge and take it with you when buying a replacement to make sure it is the correct size and 'hand'. Ceramic taps can also drip if the seal at the base of the cartridge has perished. Replace it if necessary (see page 39).

**4** Unscrew or lever off the old washer and replace it with a new one the correct size for your tap. Reassemble the tap by following the steps in reverse order.

## Mixer taps

The only difference between a mixer tap and a non-rising spindle tap is that the hot and cold water share the same outlet. In a kitchen mixer, shown here, the spout has two separate water channels for hot and cold water. The two jets of water mix only as they leave the outlet because it is against water regulations to mix cold water from the mains (as supplied to kitchen taps) with hot water from a water cylinder. This is because the pressure on the mains supply can vary and under certain conditions could draw back non-drinking water from the cylinder into the mains supply.

Mixer units for use on baths and basins can merge water supplies within the tap body as long as the cold water is coming from a water tank, not directly from the rising main supply. If the cold water is mains-fed, a back-flow prevention device must always be fitted on the cold water supply pipe.

## Mixer tap: replacing spout O-rings

**1** Turn off both the mixer taps and twist the spout to align it with the body of the taps. If there is a small grub screw behind the unit in the tap body, unscrew it. Pull the spout upwards to remove it from the body of the tap.

**2** Make a note of the position of the O-rings and prise them off using a flat head screwdriver. Smear the replacement O-rings with silicone grease before fitting them, and reassemble the tap.

Outlet

Hot water channel

Spout

Hot and cold water mix as they leave tap

Cold water channel

Headgear

Top plate

Head

Headgear

O-ring seal

## Ceramic disc taps

This type of tap operates on a different principle from conventional taps with washers and spindles. Positioned within the body of the tap is a cartridge containing a pair of ceramic discs, each with two holes in it. One disc is fixed in position; the other rotates when the handle is turned. As the movable disc rotates, the holes in it line up with the holes in the fixed one and water flows through them and out through the spout.

When the tap is turned off, the movable disc rotates so that the holes no longer align. A rubber seal at the bottom of the cartridge helps to keep the tap watertight when it is closed. Unlike conventional taps that go round and round several times, these discs move only a quarter turn from closed to fully open.

The cartridges are not interchangeable between hot and cold; they are designed as right or left-handed, depending on their position in the tap. Always make sure you know which one you need when buying a replacement.

## Cleaning or replacing ceramic disc cartridges

**1** Turn off the water supply, pull off the tap handles (it may be necessary to unscrew a small grub screw on each) and use a spanner to unscrew the headgear section. Carefully remove the ceramic disc cartridges. Check both cartridges for dirt and wear and tear. If they are worn, replace with new cartridges to suit the tap unit. Make sure the hot and cold cartridges are fitted in the correct apertures.

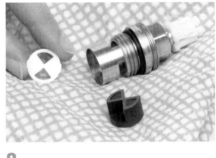

**2** If the cartridges are dirty, clean them with a damp cloth. Replace the rubber seal at the same time if it is worn. Replace the cartridge in the tap unit, fitting the hot and cold into the corresponding taps.

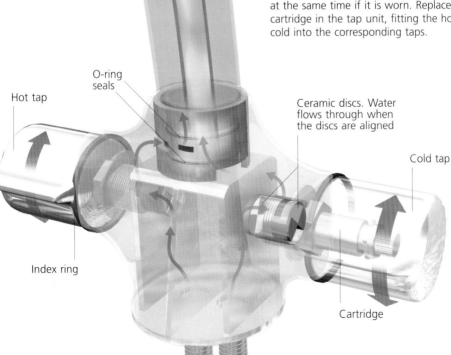

Spout

O-ring seals

Hot tap

Index ring

Ceramic discs. Water flows through when the discs are aligned

Cold tap

Cartridge

# Toilets

The basic design of the one-piece ceramic toilet has changed little in more than 100 years. Clean water is stored in a cistern above the bowl and released to flush the toilet. The water is channelled around the rim, rinsing waste matter out of the bowl and into the drainage system.

The most common problems with WCs are that the WC will not flush, that water runs continuously into the pan or that water runs continuously into the cistern and out through the overflow pipe. Most of these problems are relatively easily to fix.

Maintenance is important in hard-water areas, where limescale can build up in the cistern and around the rim of the bowl. Limescale can inhibit the flushing mechanism, while a build-up in the bowl encourages the growth of bacteria.

## MAINTENANCE

### ONCE A MONTH

Descale toilet bowl under rim *Squirt proprietary toilet cleaning product around rim and leave according to manufacturer's instructions. Flush toilet and brush away residue with a toilet brush.*

### ONCE A YEAR

Check for limescale in cistern *This can block siphon valve. Cut off water supply to cistern, flush toilet and scoop out flakes of limescale.* Check for limescale under rim of bowl *This can inhibit flow of water (see page 42).*

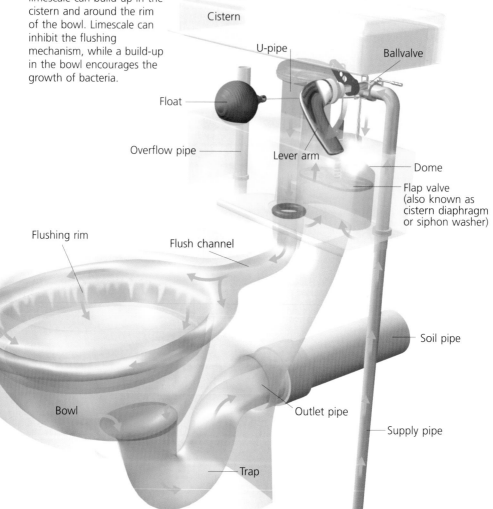

Cistern

U-pipe

Ballvalve

Float

Overflow pipe

Lever arm

Dome

Flap valve
(also known as
cistern diaphragm
or siphon washer)

Flushing rim

Flush channel

Soil pipe

Bowl

Outlet pipe

Supply pipe

Trap

## A push-button or 'European' cistern

Many modern slimline WC cisterns are too small to accommodate a traditional ball float-operated inlet valve and siphon flush mechanism, operated by a lever and float arm (see opposite).

Instead, the inlet valve is either a Torbeck valve – a modified diaphragm type with a very short float arm and miniature float (below) – or an ingenious vertical valve with a float cup that fits round the central column of the valve body. Both are quiet in operation, although the float-cup valve can be slow to refill the cistern if it is supplied with water from a storage tank, rather than being plumbed in directly to the mains.

In these slimline mechanisms, the traditional siphon flushing method is replaced by a plastic valve-operated flush mechanism that is activated by a top-mounted push button in the cistern lid. The mechanism also incorporates an integral overflow, and if the inlet valve fails for any reason, the water flows over the centre of the flush unit into the toilet bowl. This will be noticed as constantly running water in the toilet bowl and should be repaired as soon as possible.

The push button is in two parts (see box, right) and is linked to a plunger to operate the flush, rather than the conventional wire link and float arm of a traditional flushing mechanism.

### CHOOSE A DUAL-FLUSH SYSTEM TO SAVE WATER

Many modern WCs have a dual-flush cistern, allowing you to choose either a water-conserving short flush or a full flush. Conventional siphon-flush cisterns (far left) have a hole in the side of the dome; if the flush lever is released immediately, the hole lets in air after 4 litres of water have been siphoned. If the control is held down, it temporarily plugs the hole, allowing a double flush.

Push-button WCs may have a button in two parts (above). Depress one part for a low-volume flush and the other (or both, on some models) for a full-volume flush.

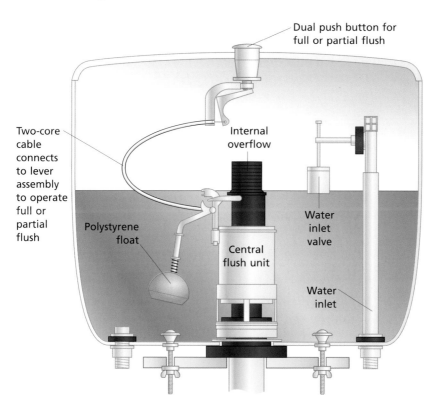

Dual push button for full or partial flush

Two-core cable connects to lever assembly to operate full or partial flush

Polystyrene float

Internal overflow

Central flush unit

Water inlet valve

Water inlet

## HOW A CISTERN WORKS

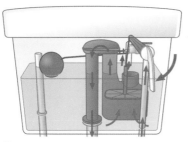

**1** An inverted U-pipe is linked to the flush pipe into the pan, and at the other end opens out into a dome (siphon). When flushed, a lift rod raises a plate in the dome and throws water over the U-bend.

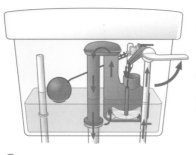

**2** Openings in the plate are covered by a plastic flap valve held flat by the weight of the water. As water falls down the flush pipe, it creates a partial vacuum, sucking water through the plate and raising the flap valve.

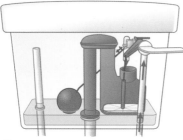

**3** The base of the dome is just above the cistern bottom. When the water level falls below the dome base, air breaks the siphonic action and stops the flush. As the cistern refills, the float lifts the inlet valve arm. When the arm reaches the top of its travel, the inlet valve closes to stop water entering. Some cisterns use a quieter Torbeck valve, which has a small cylinder in place of the ball float.

## Removing limescale from the toilet bowl

**1** Hold a small mirror under the rim of the bowl to check for limescale deposits. Clean with toilet descaler and brush.

**2** If the limescale is difficult to remove, pass a descaling product through the cistern several times. Also, squirt it under the rim and leave for several hours, or overnight, to dissolve the deposits. Clean off with a brush.

### SAFETY WARNING

Do not mix toilet descalers or rim cleaners with bleach. This can produce chlorine, which is a poisonous gas.

## FAULT DIAGNOSIS

### TOILET NOT FLUSHING CORRECTLY

Bowl not level *Check and correct if necessary.*
Flap valve (cistern diaphragm) failing *Call plumber to replace flap valve.*

### TOILET NOT FLUSHING AT ALL

Cistern not refilling properly *Check level of float on ballvalve and adjust if necessary.*
Flap valve (cistern diaphragm) failing *Call plumber to replace flap valve.*

### WATER COMING FROM OVERFLOW

Ballvalve arm closing at wrong height *Adjust level of float arm.*
Ballvalve faulty *Replace valve.*
Float punctured *Replace float.*

### CONTINUOUS SIPHONING

Debris or limescale in cistern *Turn off water supply to toilet, empty cistern and scoop out flakes of limescale and grit.*
Toilet filling too fast *If cistern fills too fast, siphoning effect may not be interrupted by air entering siphon dome, and water entering from inlet valve will continue to be drawn into bowl. If an isolating valve is fitted on supply pipe, close it slightly to reduce supply pressure. If no valve is present, fit narrower seating within inlet valve.*

### SWIVELLING SEAT

Seat broken *Replace seat.*
Loose nuts *Tighten wing nuts under the back of bowl.*

### NOISY REFILL

Portsmouth ballvalve fitted *Replace with more modern diaphragm-type valve.*

### HANDLE TURNS (OR BUTTON PUSHES DOWN) BUT NO FLUSH

Broken link *Make temporary repair with coat-hanger wire if you can. Then replace link.*
Flap valve (cistern diaphragm) failed *Call a plumber to replace valve.*

### LEAKING BEHIND TOILET

Toilet worked loose *Make sure bowl is screwed down firmly.*
Faulty bowl connector *Check seals on bowl connector. Replace if necessary.*

### LEAKING ON INLET TO BALLVALVE

Loose nut *Tighten with adjustable spanner. If this fails, turn off water supply to toilet and flush. Then unscrew external nut on ballvalve, clean threads and re-wrap with PTFE tape (thread seal tape). Tighten nut again.*

### WATER RISING UP BOWL ON FLUSHING

Toilet outlet pipe blocked on washdown bowl *Unblock toilet using plunger.*
Toilet outlet pipe blocked in siphonic bowl *Pour bucket of warm water into bowl. If this fails, use auger to dislodge blockage.*

### CONDENSATION ON CISTERN

Inadequate ventilation *Make sure bathroom is ventilated and fit an extractor fan, if necessary. Condensation is a problem primarily for cisterns supplied by water directly from rising main because this water is colder than that supplied from water tank in loft.*

## Clearing a blocked trap and outlet pipe

When a toilet is flushed, the two streams of water, one from each side of the rim, should flow equally to meet at the front. The water should leave the pan smoothly, not eddying like a whirlpool. If the cistern is working properly but the bowl fails to clear, something is obstructing either the flush inlet or the pan outlet. If the flush water rises almost to the pan rim, then ebbs away very slowly, there is probably a blockage in the pan outlet (or possibly in the soil stack or drain into which it discharges).

You can often clear a blockage by pouring several buckets of warm water into the pan. Alternatively you may need to use a plunger or an auger to dislodge it.

> ### CLEARING A BLOCKAGE
>
> To increase the force when freeing a blockage, stand on a chair and pour a bucket of warm water in one go into the bowl.

**1** To clear the pan, take the plunger and push it sharply onto the bottom of the pan to cover the outlet. Then pump the handle up and down two or three times. If you don't have a plunger, try using a mop.

**2** If this does not clear the pan, use a flexible drain auger to probe the outlet and trap. As you insert the auger, turn it slowly. If you meet hard resistance, turn the auger back and forth to move it past the trap. When you meet soft resistance, push and pull gently to dislodge the blockage. Flush the bowl with a bucket of water.

**3** If the blockage persists, you will need to contact a drain-rodding company to get the underground drain checked and cleared.

**4** Flush the cistern to check that water is entering the pan properly, with streams from each side of the rim flowing equally to meet at the front.

**5** If the flow into the pan is poor or uneven, use a mirror to examine the flushing rim. Use your fingers to dislodge flakes of limescale or debris from the outlets that may be obstructing the flow of the flush water.

## Levelling the bowl

Use a spirit-level to check whether the rim of the toilet is level from side to side and front to back. If it isn't, loosen the nuts or screws holding the bowl down and level the bowl using strips of vinyl tile, thin strips of rubber or wood (shims) or sealant. Screw the bowl down firmly again.

## Replacing a seat

**1** Undo the plastic wing-nuts under the rear of the toilet bowl and remove the broken seat. Clean around the bolt holes and make sure the area is rinsed properly and dry. Place the new seat in position.

**2** Make sure the supplied washers are fitted above and below the bowl, on both bolts. Finger-tighten the wing-nuts. Then check the seat is centred on the bowl. Tighten the nuts fully.

### QUICK FIX FOR A LEAKING BALL-VALVE FLOAT

If your float is taking in water it will not operate correctly, and may not be able to rise far enough to close the inlet valve. Make a temporary repair by tying up the float arm to cut off the water supply. Unscrew and remove the ball float and drain out the water inside it (enlarge the hole with a sharp knife if necessary). Replace the float then slip a plastic freezer bag over it, squeeze out the air and tie it securely to the float arm with string. Release the arm and allow the cistern to refill.

## Replacing a broken link to the ballvalve

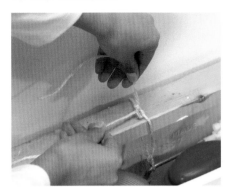

**1** Turn off the water supply to the toilet and flush it by pulling up on the rod protruding from the dome of the siphon. If you cannot turn the water off, place a wooden batten across the cistern and tie the ballvalve arm up.

**2** Remove the broken sections of link from the ends of the rods and discard. Then fit the new link between the siphon rod and the nylon connector bar.

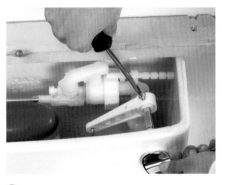

**3** Push the other end of the bar onto the lever arm rod. Make sure the arm is in the 'rest' position, and tighten the retaining screw. Then untie the float from the wooden batten and allow the cistern to fill.

# Electric shower

Most electric showers are fed directly from the rising main, heating water as it passes through the unit. The most common problem encountered with electric showers is poor water flow due to limescale building up within the unit or the shower head. This is particularly prevalent in hard-water areas but regular maintenance should help to prevent it.

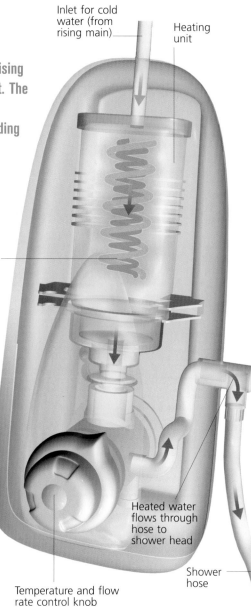

Inlet for cold water (from rising main)

Heating unit

Shower head

Heating element

Heated water flows through hose to shower head

Temperature and flow rate control knob

Shower hose

Shower units are connected to a dedicated circuit from the mains electric supply, so before attempting any repairs or maintenance always ensure that the mains supply is switched off. Electric showers use heating elements to heat water as it passes through the unit in much the same way that water in a hot water tank is heated by contact with the heating coil (see page 58). The temperature of the water is controlled by adjusting the flow rate: the faster the water runs past the heating elements, the cooler it will be. Limescale build up will reduce the efficiency of the heating elements (much like a furred up kettle) as well as reducing the flow of water through the unit and shower head.

Many problems are easily remedied, but anything that requires opening the shower unit itself is generally best left to a qualified electrician.

| MAINTENANCE |
| --- |
| **ONCE A MONTH** |
| Descale shower head *Also clean outside of shower unit using a non-abrasive sponge and a mild detergent. Make sure limescale isn't building up around knobs and fittings. Wipe down with descaler.* |
| **ONCE A YEAR** |
| Clean shower pump filters *If shower is a power shower, clean the plastic filters located within the hot and cold pump inlet connections.* |

## POWER SHOWER

Where the mains water pressure is low a power shower, which has an internal or external electric pump, will boost the flow. These units mix hot and cold water from your hot water cylinder and cold water cistern to achieve the desired temperature.

## FAULT DIAGNOSIS

### WATER KEEPS GOING COLD

Faulty thermostat *Contact qualified repairer.*
Water pressure dropping below atmospheric pressure *This may be due to people flushing toilet or local variations. Fit power shower.*

### NO HOT WATER FROM INSTANT UNIT

Thermal safety cut-out tripped *Allow shower to run cold until cut-out is reset. If this happens repeatedly, water pressure is too low.*
Elements overheating *This could be caused by build-up of scale on elements. Contact qualified repairer.*
Thermostat faulty *Contact qualified repairer.*

### NO HOT WATER FROM POWER SHOWER

No hot water left in hot water cylinder *Heat water.*
Blocked pump inlet filters *Clean or replace.*
Pump drawing in air *See 'Pump noisy' (top right).*

### LEAKS FROM UNIT OR HOSE

Internal valves worn *Contact qualified repairer.*
Washers worn or damaged *Replace washers in ends of hoses with identical parts. (Many manufacturers sell a spares kits with a diagram showing how to fit parts.)*

### FLOW FROM SHOWER HEAD IS LOW

Limescale build-up *Descale.*
Local mains pressure down *Check pressure from taps. Try again when pressure restored.*
Stoptap not open fully *Locate main stoptap and open to one quarter turn less than fully open.*
Pump not functioning *Check power supply.*

## FAULT DIAGNOSIS CONT.

### PUMP NOISY (IF FITTED)

Limescale or debris in mechanism *Descale and clean pump if possible. If not, contact qualified repairer.*
Air being drawn into pump *If pressure on inlet is not sufficient and water is very hot, a problem known as cavitation can occur. To solve problem, increase size of pipes (22mm diameter for inlet and 15mm for outlet is best).*
Bearings worn *Contact qualified repairer.*

## DESCALING A SHOWER HEAD

**1** Unscrew the shower head. There may be a tool supplied with your shower; use a screwdriver if there is a central screw. If the rose does not unscrew, remove the whole head from the hose. Pour white vinegar or descaler through or over the head.

**2** Scrub the rose with an old nailbrush or washing-up brush. If the holes are badly blocked, soak the head in a proprietary descaler according to the manufacturer's instructions or leave it overnight in undiluted white vinegar.

**3** Reattach the shower head to the hose, and turn the shower on for a few minutes on its cold setting to rinse out the limescale and any remaining descaler or vinegar. Repeat this process several times to make sure all the cleaning product has been rinsed away.

# Waste water problems

**Houses have either a two-pipe drainage system or one drain pipe, called a single stack system. In either system there is the potential for blockages and nasty smells.**

Every bath, basin or sink in the house is fitted with a trap – a bend in the outlet pipe below the plughole (see right). This holds sufficient water to stop gases from the drains entering the house and causing an unpleasant smell. Traps are hot spots for blockages but each trap has some means of access for clearing out debris. All WC pans have built-in traps (U-bends).

Below ground, household waste pipes are channelled through an inspection chamber near the house to the main drain, which runs into the water company's sewer.

## Single stack system

Modern houses have a single stack drainage system. Waste from all sinks and WCs is carried underground by a single vertical pipe known as a soil stack. This pipe may be installed inside the house and its vented top extends above the roof.

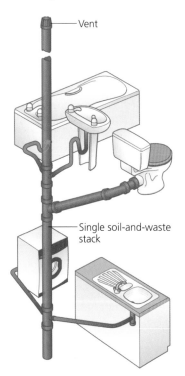

Vent

Single soil-and-waste stack

## Two-pipe system

Most houses built before the mid-1960s have what is known as a two-pipe drainage system for the disposal of waste water (see below). A vertical soil stack fixed to an outside wall carries waste from upstairs WCs to an underground drain.

The open top of the soil stack – the vent – extends above the eaves and allows the escape of sewer gases. It is protected from birds with a metal or wire mesh guard. Ground floor WCs have an outlet direct into the underground drain.

A second outside pipe – the waste pipe – takes used water from upstairs baths, basins and showers via an open hopper head to empty into a ground-level gully. Water from the kitchen sink also runs into the gully.

A blockage can arise at any point in the waste water system. The method for dealing with the blockage depends on where it occurs.

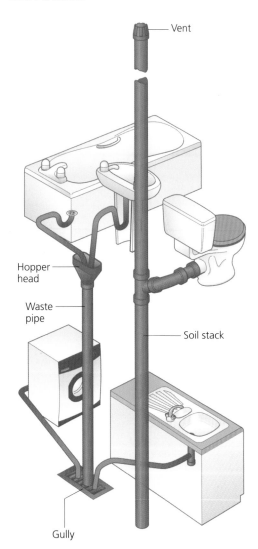

Vent

Hopper head

Waste pipe

Soil stack

Gully

## Septic tanks

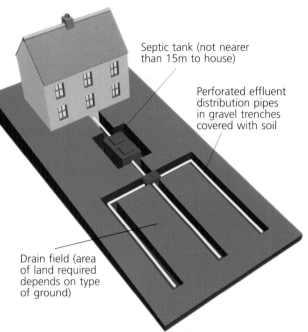

Septic tank (not nearer than 15m to house)

Perforated effluent distribution pipes in gravel trenches covered with soil

Drain field (area of land required depends on type of ground)

A septic tank is often used in rural areas where there is no access to a communal sewerage system. Matter that is lighter than water (scum) floats to the top, while matter that is heavier than water (sludge) falls to the floor. As new water enters the tank, some of the existing water is displaced into a series of perforated pipes in the drain field. Non-biodegradable products, such as tampons, can block the system, and many household chemicals can interfere with the bacteriological action of the tank.

### TRAPS AND U-BENDS

Plastic traps are 'U', 'P' or bottle-shaped. As water fills up past the bend in the 'U' it spills over the edge and drains away through a connecting pipe. The water forms a barrier, preventing noxious gases coming up the pipe from the drains.

### MAINTENANCE

#### EVERY TWO TO THREE MONTHS

Check washing machine and dishwasher non-return valves for blockages

#### ONCE EVERY SIX MONTHS

Clean waste pipes and traps *Add a small amount of chemical drain cleaner (not with septic tanks). Pour down plugholes of sinks and basins. Take care as these chemicals can be poisonous. Use a product designed to break down fats and grease.* Check outside grates over gullies *Clear blockages of leaves, dirt and garden debris.*

#### ONCE A YEAR

Have septic tanks emptied and cleaned *The proportion of effluent, sludge and scum must be carefully balanced for the tank to work efficiently.*

### SIMPLE STEPS TO AVOID BLOCKAGES

Put only waste water down a drain. If possible, keep grease, ground coffee, hair and fluff out of the drain. Try to remove any build-up of hair in basin or shower wastes before it becomes a blockage. A wet and dry vacuum cleaner is a good tool for this job.

Never flush tampons or nappies down the toilet.

Never pour fat down a sink in case the fat solidifies when it returns to room temperature. Allow fat to solidify in an old container and throw it out with the rubbish. If you accidentally pour fat down a sink, immediately squirt in some washing up liquid and flush with very hot water. Hot air from a hair dryer will also melt congealed fat in a trap.

Keep plugholes clean with a regular application of bleach.

## FAULT DIAGNOSIS

### WATER NOT DRAINING FROM SINK OR BATH

Blocked waste pipe *Clear blockage with plunger. If no plunger is available, undo trap connections and clear blockage manually.*

### WATER DRAINING SLOWLY FROM SINK OR BATH

Partially blocked plughole or waste pipe *Pick out dirt and debris from plughole or use a chemical drain cleaner. Chemical drain cleaners should not be used with septic tanks.*

### TOILET BLOCKED

Toilet blocked *Use a toilet plunger to clear the blockage. Make sure rim of plunger is below surface of the water and pump 10 times before removing abruptly. If this fails, use an auger to dislodge the obstacle. Turn the handle slowly clockwise as you push towards the blockage.*

### BAD SMELLS

Leak in system *Check under sinks and bath for leaks. Try tightening trap nuts. Replace seals if worn.*
Blockage further down the system, beyond house *Contact drain and pipe cleaning company to rod the drains.*
Trap seal losing water *Consult qualified plumber or fit deeper traps.*

### SMELLS FROM WASHING MACHINE

Waste water entering washing machine *Check the outlet pipe is fitted properly.*
Waste hose at wrong angle *This should be higher than sink overflow to stop water from the sink flowing back into washing machine.*
Blocked non-return valve *Remove fluff and debris (see above right).*

## Clearing non-return valves

**1** Locate the non-return valve behind or near the washing machine or dishwasher. The drain hose will be attached to it. Unscrew the plastic retaining collar that holds the hose coupling to the valve.

**2** Lift out the valve and remove any dirt or fluff that may be blocking it. Retighten the retaining collar firmly by hand.

### DISMANTLING WASTE PIPES

Waste pipes joined with push-fit or screw-up connectors are easily taken apart when there is a blockage that you cannot free with a plunger. If your waste pipe is easy to access, this is an alternative to buying or hiring an auger. Start dismantling the pipe at the outlet end, where it discharges into an outdoor gully, for example, and work your way back until you locate the blockage. Put a bucket under the end of the pipe and use a length of stiff wire to dislodge the blockage.

Reassemble the pipe run, making sure that any sealing rings inside screw-up fittings are correctly positioned, or the joints will leak.

# Clearing a blocked waste pipe

**1** Block the overflow with a wet cloth and fill the sink to cover the rim of the plunger. Allow any air to escape. Then pump the plunger up and down 10 times.

**3** Allow water to drain, and probe using bent wire inside the pipe to remove any clogged material. Clean and replace trap.

**2** If this does not work, place a bucket under the trap and remove its plug, or unscrew the bottom of a bottle trap. If necessary, remove the whole trap.

**4** Another method is to feed an auger through the plughole. Turn the handle clockwise to get past the trap. When you feel soft resistance, work the auger back and forth. Flush with hot water.

# Cleaning a waste pipe from a bath or basin

**1** Allow remaining water to drain, then smear petroleum jelly on the rim of the plughole. This is to protect the finish against the harsh chemicals required to clear a drain.

**2** Pour chemical cleaner (caustic soda or enzyme) down the plughole according to manufacturer's instructions. Rinse with fresh water. Never use a plunger immediately after cleaning with chemicals.

# Central heating

Most central heating systems warm the rooms of a house by passing hot water through a system of pipes and radiators. The type of central heating system you have may depend on the age of your house. It is important to understand how it works.

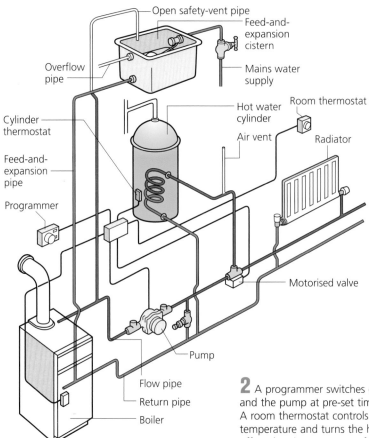

Open safety-vent pipe
Feed-and-expansion cistern
Overflow pipe
Mains water supply
Cylinder thermostat
Hot water cylinder
Room thermostat
Air vent
Radiator
Feed-and-expansion pipe
Programmer
Motorised valve
Pump
Flow pipe
Return pipe
Boiler

## A typical pumped system

There are many ways of heating the water that passes through radiators to warm a house, but it is usually heated by a boiler, which switches on automatically at certain times of day.

**1** A room thermostat turns on the pump (or opens a motorised valve) and the boiler. The pump drives water around the system. The motorised valve opens and closes the circuits to the radiators and hot water cylinder as required by the thermostats. The water in the central heating system is separate from that supplied to the hot taps.

**2** A programmer switches on the boiler and the pump at pre-set times of the day. A room thermostat controls the room temperature and turns the heating on and off as the air temperature falls and rises. Water is heated by the boiler and flows through pipes to the radiators. When the air temperature reaches the required level, the valve is closed or the pump is switched off.

**3** The same water is constantly circulated around the system. In an open system (above), in case of leakage or evaporation, the water is topped up from a feed-and-expansion cistern. This cistern also allows room for the water to expand as it heats up from cold.

**4** An open-ended pipe, called the open safety-vent pipe, provides an escape route for steam and excess pressure if the boiler should overheat.

## Gravity fed

In some older central heating systems and in solid fuel systems, water is circulated by gravity. When water is heated it expands and hot water weighs less than cold water.

**1** Hot water rises up a large pipe from the boiler to the hot water cylinder. Cooled water descends down the return pipe, pushing the lighter hot water up the flow pipe.

**2** A pump, controlled by a programmer and room thermostat, drives water around the radiators. Gravity circulation is reliable as it needs no mechanical assistance, but it requires larger 28mm pipes.

Hot water cylinder

Hot water rises

Cold water falls

Pump

Boiler

## A sealed system

A sealed central heating system has an expansion vessel (closed pressure vessel) instead of an expansion cistern, and a pressure relief valve instead of a safety-vent pipe. The valve should be set permanently to 3 bar. Any water lost through minor leaks is topped up from the mains. Sealed systems are ideal for flats, where it is difficult to locate tanks.

**1** A thermostat opens the motorised valve, which controls the circuits to the radiators.

**2** The valve turns on the pump to drive water around the system, and starts up the boiler.

**3** The boiler has an over-heat cut-out to prevent the system boiling should the standard thermostat fail. Increasingly the old sealed systems built from individual components are being replaced by modern combination boilers (see right).

High-temperature safety cut-out

Safety valve

Closed pressure vessel

Mains filling point

**Modern boilers** The essential components of a sealed system are now usually housed inside the boiler. As well as saving space because of the lack of a feed-and-expansion cistern, a combination boiler also has the advantage that no hot water cylinder is needed as the boiler heats mains water and delivers hot water directly to the taps.

<table>
<tr><td colspan="1">

**MAINTENANCE**

**MONTHLY**

Check and bleed radiators if required *If radiators are hot at bottom and cold at top, they need bleeding (page 56).*

**EVERY YEAR (BEFORE SWITCHING ON HEATING FOR THE WINTER)**

Test the water in a central heating system for corrosion *Internal corrosion can be extremely expensive to repair.*
Check the lagging *Make sure all the pipes in the loft are insulated before winter. If you're taking a short break, leave the heating on a low setting while you are away.*
Have the boiler serviced. *This should be carried out by a qualified professional.*
</td></tr>
</table>

## Checking and inhibiting corrosion

**1** Drain off some water from the drain valve at the boiler into a glass jar. Place two bright (non-galvanised) nails in the jar. Put the lid on and leave for a week or so. If, after a week, the nails are badly corroded and the water has changed to a rusty orange colour, then there is corrosion in the system. Some black deposits are acceptable.

## Curing a leaking bleed valve

Use a radiator drain key to tighten the valve. If the leak continues, turn off the handwheel and lockshield valves at the bottom of the radiator where the water pipes enter and leave. Then unscrew the leaking valve and replace it.

**2** Corrosion inhibitors can be injected directly into the valve at the top of each radiator – follow the manufacturer's instructions carefully. Otherwise, add a corrosion inhibitor/antifreeze to the feed and expansion cistern in the loft. Tie up the ballvalve arm, drain off some water from the system, and add the inhibitor/antifreeze to the tank (make sure you add the mixture to the central heating feed and expansion tank). Then release the ballvalve arm. Refer to the manufacturer's instructions for the correct amount and specific details.

# Fixing a leaking radiator valve

**1** Turn off the valves at each end of the radiator. Make a note of the number of turns required to turn the lockshield valve off. Put a towel and a bowl under the valve to catch water, and have a bucket and a second bowl ready.

**3** Open the air vent using a flat tip screwdriver or a radiator key (depending on the make of valve). This will allow the rest of the water to flow out into the bowl.

**2** Use an adjustable spanner to turn the union nut (the nut attached to the radiator) anticlockwise (when looking from the radiator to the valve) until the joint is loose. To prevent bending the pipe, counterbalance the force by holding the nut just below the valve with a Stilson wrench.

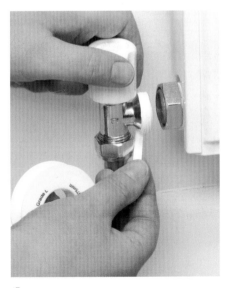

**4** Wind PTFE tape tightly around the thread on the valve tail to create a water-tight seal. Start at the end and make a 50 per cent overlap on each turn. Then, retighten the nut firmly over the tape. Open the lockshield and handwheel valves and allow the radiator to fill with water. When water starts to run out of the bleed valve, close it.

## FAULT DIAGNOSIS

### NO HEAT OR WATER

Timer and thermostats set incorrectly *Make sure that the programmer is on, that all thermostats are set high enough and that any heating controls on the boiler are turned up.*

Problem in valve motor *Check motorised valve by sliding the manual lever. If difficult to move, call heating engineer.*

Jammed pump *Tap pump gently with a mallet. If this doesn't work, try to start pump manually by turning the screw on the front of the pump housing. If neither works, call heating engineer.*

Pilot light gone out *Re-ignite pilot light following the instructions in boiler manufacturer's manual.*

No gas *Check other gas appliances, such as cooker. If no supply, call gas company. If gas is just not reaching boiler, call heating engineer.*

### CENTRAL HEATING WORKING BUT NO HOT WATER

Check thermostat on hot water cylinder is set to 60°C *If too low, then valve will not open to route hot water through heater coil in cylinder.*

Bleed air-release valve next to hot water cylinder *This can usually be found on pipe which feeds hot water to heater coil.*

### LEAK IN SYSTEM

Leaking pipe joint *Most pipe joints are compression fittings. This means they can be tightened slightly. This will stop most leaks.*

Leaking radiator valve *If leak is from beneath valve, call plumber. If between valve and radiator, then use PTFE tape to seal the joint (page 55). If leak is from under cap, repack the gland (see facing page).*

Leaking bleed valve *Tighten bleed valve or replace (page 54).*

## PROTECT THE SYSTEM AGAINST FROST DAMAGE

An anti-corrosive antifreeze can be added to the feed and expansion cistern to prevent heating pipes freezing. You can also fit a frost thermostat to the heating system. This overrides the system's settings and turns the heating on if the air temperature approaches zero.

## Bleeding a radiator

Make sure the central heating has been off for at least an hour. Use a radiator bleed key to release air from the system. On some radiators, a flat tip screwdriver may be required instead of the key. Turn the key anticlockwise (no more than a quarter turn), and hold a cloth under the valve to catch any drips. Air should come out with a hissing noise. When water starts to come out, close the valve and wipe the area dry. Do this to all the radiators in the house.

If no water emerges from the valve, the hole in the air vent may be blocked, or the system may be short of water. Try bleeding another radiator on the same floor. If this has water in it, return to the original radiator and unblock the hole. Turn off the radiator valves, open the vent and remove the needle inside. Put it somewhere safe. Use a length of stiff wire to clear the blockage, pushing it back into the radiator, replace the needle and open the radiator valves. Be prepared to close the bleed vent: water should begin to flow out.

If no water came out of the second radiator, check that there is water in the feed-and-expansion tank. If it is empty, refill it by pressing down on the arm of the float valve.

## Repacking a radiator gland

Radiator valves, especially the cheaper ones, often weep around the spindles. Before replacing the valve, it is worth trying to repack the gland to cure the problem. You will need a roll of PTFE tape and some silicon grease.

**1** Turn off the handwheel valve and close the lockshield valve at the other end of the radiator. Remove the cap from the leaking valve and use an adjustable spanner to undo the small gland nut.

**2** Slide the nut up out of the way. Pull a length of PTFE tape into a string and wrap this around the spindle four or five times.

**3** Use a small screwdriver to push the tape down firmly into the valve body.

**4** Smear on silicone grease using a wooden spatula, and retighten the gland nut using the adjustable spanner. Replace the head and turn the valve back on.

### BANGING PIPES

Banging noises in the pipes may be due to overheating. Check that the boiler thermostat is working properly. Rattling copper pipework can be remedied by securing the pipes at intervals with plastic push-fit brackets. Pipes running through joists under floorboards can be quietened using lagging or felt.

# Immersion heater

An immersion heater is used to heat water when the central heating boiler is switched off – in summer, for example – or when a boost of hot water is required.

Mains power heats the central element, which comprises a wire encased in mineral insulation. Heat is conducted from the element to the water, which rises to the top of the cylinder as it heats up.

When the thermostat sensor detects that the water is at the set temperature, it turns the element off. Hot water is drawn off from the top of the cylinder, and cold enters at the bottom to replace it. When the temperature of the water drops, the thermostat turns the element back on. The element is powered via a 20A double-pole (DP) switch, and must be on its own electrical circuit connected directly to the consumer unit. Heat-resistant flex links the heater to this on/off switch.

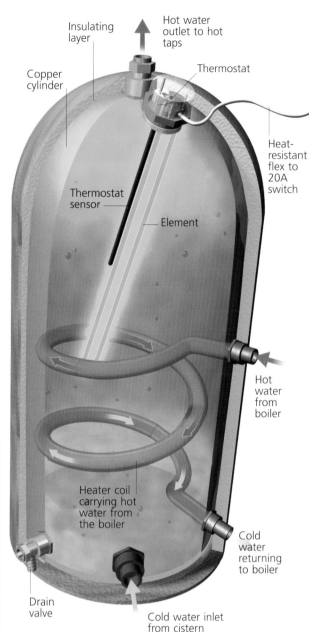

Insulating layer
Hot water outlet to hot taps
Copper cylinder
Thermostat
Heat-resistant flex to 20A switch
Thermostat sensor
Element
Hot water from boiler
Heater coil carrying hot water from the boiler
Cold water returning to boiler
Drain valve
Cold water inlet from cistern

## FAULT DIAGNOSIS

### NO HEAT

Faulty element *Replace immersion heater.*
Faulty thermostat *Turn off power at local switch, then remove immersion heater's top cover, as in step 3 (right). Disconnect cables and replace thermostat.*

### WATER NOT HOT ENOUGH

Thermostat set too low *Adjust temperature to around 60°C.*
Faulty thermostat *See above.*
Sediment in cylinder *Remove sediment. (See maintenance.)*

### NOISE WHEN HEATING

Mineral deposits on element *Replace immersion heater.*
Sediment in cylinder *See maintenance.*

## MAINTENANCE

### WHEN REQUIRED

Remove sediment *Turn off the cold water supply to the cylinder, disconnect the hot feed pipe and add a descaling chemical to cylinder and leave for 24 hours. Drain cylinder fully, turn on the cold water supply and refill. See steps 1, 2 and 7 (right) to drain cylinder.*

## SAFETY WARNING

Always turn off the double-pole isolating switch when working on an immersion heater or its thermostat. Make sure all other water heating devices, for example a central heating boiler, are turned off before draining the cylinder.

## Replacing the heater

**1** Turn off the cold water supply to the hot water cylinder. If your immersion heater is on top of the cylinder, turn on a hot tap until no more water comes out then go to step 3. Otherwise, attach a hose to the drain valve (which is either on the side of the cylinder as shown, or on the cold water inlet pipe) and run it to a drain.

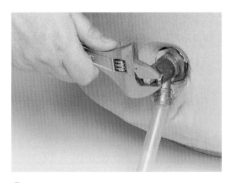

**2** Use a spanner to open the drain valve. If the nut is tight, grip the body of the drain valve with an adjustable spanner so that the whole valve does not start to turn.

**3** Turn off the power to the heater at the local switch. Remove the heater's top cover and disconnect the flex cores.

**4** Use an immersion heater spanner to unscrew the element, taking care not to split the cylinder. Then pull the heater out. If it is stuck, either apply penetrating oil and wait ten minutes or, if the cylinder has no insulation moulded round it, use a gentle flame from a blowlamp.

**5** Make sure the area around the hole is clean. Wrap PTFE tape around the threads on the new heater.

**6** Insert the new heater into the cylinder and tighten it fully with the spanner. Reconnect the flex and ensure the heater is properly earthed.

**7** Replace the heater's top cover. Close the hot tap you opened and refill the cylinder, watching carefully for any leaks, which will happen as soon as refilling starts. If you have opened the drain valve, close this as soon as clear water runs out. When the cylinder is full, turn the power back on and check for heat.

# Cylinder door lock

Nearly every front door is fitted with this type of lock. It has an ingenious mechanism, and one that is easy to put right if the flat key fails to turn.

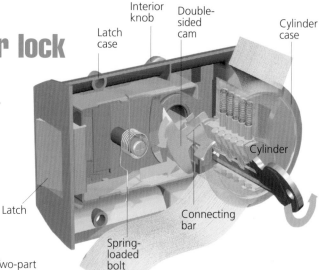

Interior knob
Double-sided cam
Cylinder case
Latch case
Cylinder
Connecting bar
Latch
Spring-loaded bolt

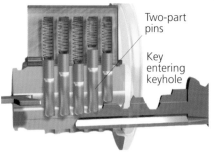

Two-part pins

Key entering keyhole

**1** As the key is pushed into the keyhole, its notched edge pushes up a series of two-part pins, the ends of which are held against each other by springs.

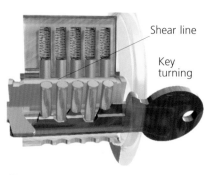

Shear line

Key turning

**2** When the key is fully in, the breaks in the tops of the pins will all coincide with the shear line between the case and cylinder, allowing the cylinder to rotate as the key is turned.

**3** The connecting bar sticking out from the end of the cylinder turns a double-sided cam, which operates a spring-loaded bolt to depress the latch.

**4** Releasing the key then reverses the whole sequence: the spring-loaded bolt pushes the latch out; the cam, connecting bar and cylinder turn; and the ends of the pins line up so that the key can be removed.

## MAINTENANCE

### WHEN REQUIRED

Lubricate cylinder and latch
*Moisture and dust can enter a lock through the keyhole, making it difficult to insert and turn the key. Use lubricant spray or powdered graphite (stocked by locksmiths) to lubricate cylinder, squirting it into keyhole. Then turn interior knob to depress latch and lubricate latch case through latch cut-out. If lock is still stiff, it is a sign that the cylinder is worn and needs replacing.*

## FAULT DIAGNOSIS

### KEY STICKS IN LOCK OR WON'T TURN

Worn cylinder *In time, the ends of the pins become worn, making it increasingly difficult to turn the key. However, as long as the interior knob is not operated by a key, you can buy just a replacement cylinder, together with new keys.*

**5** The interior knob also operates a double-sided cam to push on the spring-loaded bolt and depress the latch into its case, allowing the door to be opened.

## Replacing a cylinder

**1** Remove the latch case on the inside of the door and undo the two screw-headed bolts securing the cylinder to the mounting plate. Use the other hand to support the lock on the outside of the door, so that it does not fall out.

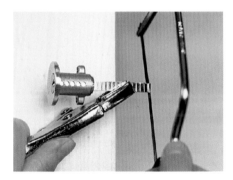

**2** Hold the connecting bar of the replacement cylinder with a wrench or pliers and cut with a junior hacksaw to same length as that on old cylinder. Some bars can be snapped to length with two pairs of pliers. File the end smooth.

**3** Slide the replacement cylinder into place and connect it to the mounting plate with the bolts, checking that the maker's name on the lock face stays upright as you tighten the bolts. Refit the latch case and make sure the new key turns smoothly to operate the lock.

## REPLACING BELL WIRE

**1** If the doorbell is mains powered, turn off the power first. If it is battery powered, remove the bell unit cover and take out the batteries. Then unscrew the bell push from the door frame. Remove the terminal screws retaining the old wire and connect a new length of wire. You may have to route the cable through a hole in the door frame first. Replace the bell push.

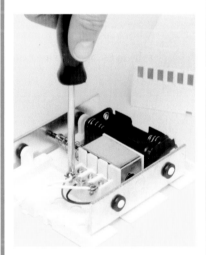

**2** Cut the new wire to the length of the old one. Make a note of the position of the connections, then remove the old wire from the bell unit, and attach the new wires to the terminals. Fix the new wire to the wall and door frame. If the bell is mains powered, replace the cover and turn on the mains power. Otherwise, replace the batteries and reattach the cover. Then test the bell push.

# Mortise door lock

You may need to replace a mortise lock if your keys have been stolen or if the door has been forced. The more levers a mortise lock has, the harder it is to pick. Typically, a mortise lock has five levers (shown below).

A mortise key has a series of notches. When the key is inserted into the keyhole and turned, these notches align with the levers inside the lock casing, which are held in place by springs.

As the key is turned, the notches raise each lever to the height of its gate. Only at this position can the stump pass the gate, freeing the bolt. The key also turns the bolt thrower, which is kept in place by a spring. The bolt thrower has a ridge (shown below in blue), which pushes the bolt out into the strike plate and keeper. The springs push the levers back down into a locked position when the bolt is fully extended. The door is now deadlocked.

Steel pins embedded in the bolt roll under a hacksaw blade, making it impossible to saw through the bolt. The casing is made of drill-resistant hardened steel. The keeper in the door frame is a steel box, which prevents an intruder forcing the bolt back into the lock.

To unlock the door, the key is turned in the opposite direction. The key raises the levers to free the bolt, which moves back.

## HOME SECURITY

Remember that a lock is only as strong as the door and frame in which it is fitted. Replace fragile or damaged wood before fitting new locks. One lock may not be enough to resist a determined intruder. It is best to fit a mortise and cylinder lock at different heights. This will spread the load of any blows to the door. Buy only locks that conform to British Standard BS 3621.

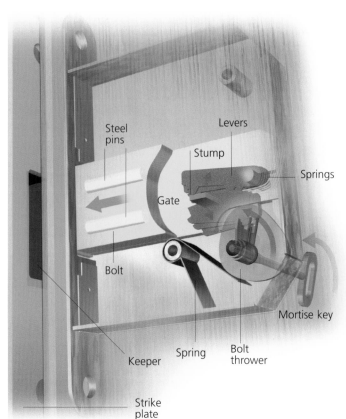

Steel pins — Levers — Stump — Springs — Gate — Bolt — Mortise key — Keeper — Spring — Bolt thrower — Strike plate

## Opening the gate

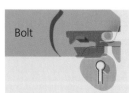

When the lock is not locked, the bolt is held in place because the stump (green) is gripped by the levers (only one lever shown).

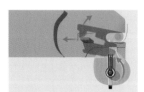

When the key is turned, the notches in the key match the shape of the levers and lift them. The bolt thrower (blue) turns and pushes the bolt out.

Once the bolt has moved into the locked position, the levers move back, making it impossible to push the bolt back into the lock.

## Replacing a mortise lock

**1** Open the door to expose the bolt and the strike plate. Unscrew the face-plate, then turn the key to operate the bolt.

| MAINTENANCE |
|---|
| **WHEN REQUIRED** |
| Lubricate mechanism *Use aerosol lubricant or powdered graphite (stocked by locksmiths) to lubricate the levers by squirting it in through the keyhole. Operate the lock a few times to dispense the lubricant.* |

| FAULT DIAGNOSIS |
|---|
| **KEY TURNS BUT BOLT WON'T MOVE** |
| Grime between levers *This prevents them from moving freely.* Lubricate levers. Worn levers *During years of use, levers can become worn, so their gates won't properly free the stump.* Replace lock. Broken springs *Replace lock.* |
| **KEY DOESN'T TURN** |
| Worn or damaged key *Get a new key cut from an unworn spare.* |

**2** Remove the key and then slide out the lock by gripping the projecting bolt with pliers and pulling outwards.

**3** Push a matching replacement lock into the door, and secure the lock and face-plate with the screws.

**4** Make sure the new key turns smoothly to operate the lock.

# Appliances

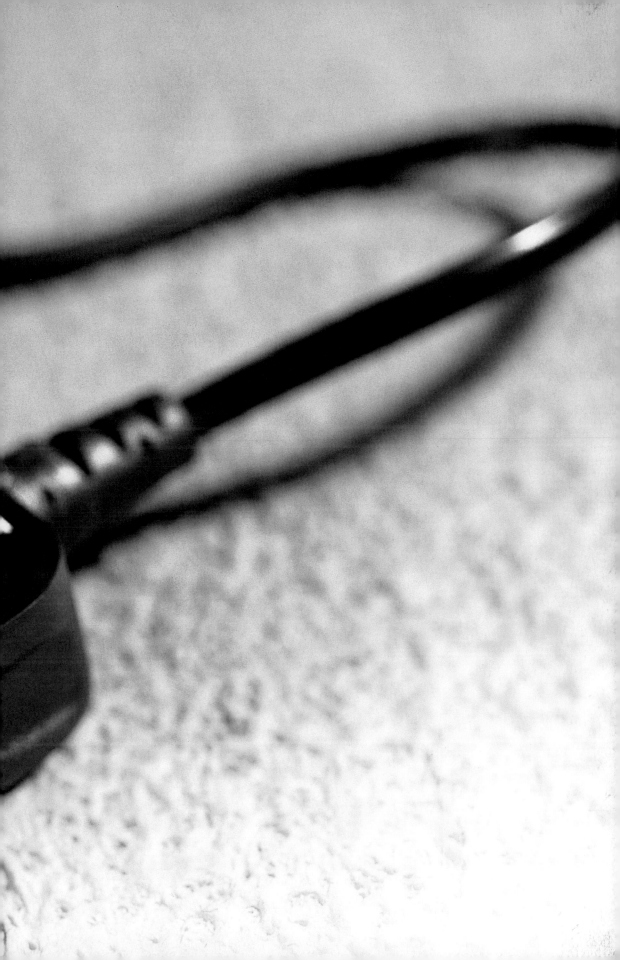

# Washing machine

Washing machines can quickly become clogged up with undissolved detergent, limescale and fluff from dirty laundry. Regular cleaning will prolong the life of your machine. Once you understand how the different parts work, maintaining and repairing your machine will be much easier.

Setting the programmer and switching on the machine activates the door interlock. On most models, once the door is shut, it cannot be opened until the programme is finished: some allow you to interrupt the

### SAFETY WARNING

Always unplug, disconnect or isolate any appliance when carrying out cleaning or maintenance.

first stage of the cycle to add a forgotten item. As soon as the door is locked, the programme begins. The inlet valves open, allowing water to flow into the drum. On the way, the water passes through the detergent tray, collecting powder or liquid. The water entering the drum compresses

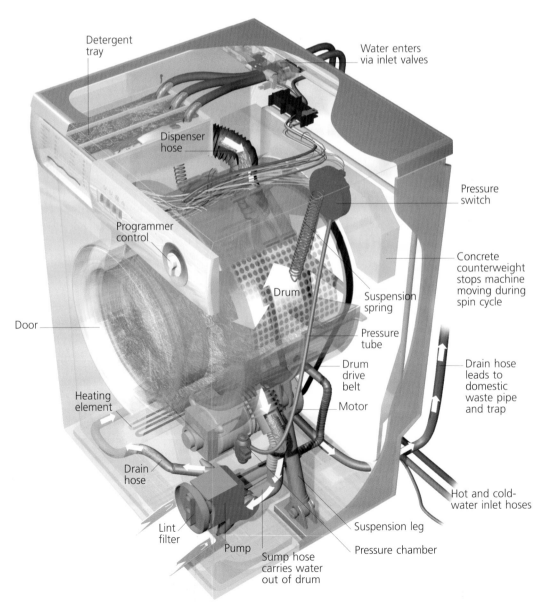

Detergent tray

Water enters via inlet valves

Dispenser hose

Pressure switch

Programmer control

Concrete counterweight stops machine moving during spin cycle

Drum

Suspension spring

Door

Pressure tube

Heating element

Drum drive belt

Motor

Drain hose leads to domestic waste pipe and trap

Drain hose

Hot and cold-water inlet hoses

Lint filter

Suspension leg

Pump

Pressure chamber

Sump hose carries water out of drum

air in a pressure chamber. This pressure is relayed along a flexible tube to a pressure switch, which shuts the inlet valves at the programmed water level.

The heating element comes on, raising the water temperature to the programmed level. On very hot washes, only the hot inlet valve may open. This reduces the time the heating element is on. However some machines, particularly in properties with combination boilers, may be plumbed in with only a cold-water supply, so that all water is heated within the machine.

The motor drives the drum to move the clothes around in the water and to spin them at high speed to dispel the water after they have been rinsed. The pump drains dirty water and rinsing water from the tub via a lint filter and the drain hose. After a hot wash, the cold inlet valve may open first to cool fabrics gradually and protect them from damage or shrinkage.

After a delay to allow the drum to stop spinning at the end of the cycle, the door lock is disengaged. The programme is now finished and the door can be opened.

## Servicing inlet hoses

Turn off the water supply and undo the hose connections at both ends – they should never be more than handtight. Remove the washers from the connections and replace if they appear worn or there is water staining around the connection points on the back of the machine.

Using pliers, carefully draw the hose filters out of the back of the valve bodies (below). Rinse filters under running water and, before refitting, remove any debris lodged in the valve inlet, making sure none of it gets pushed into the valve itself.

---

### MAINTENANCE

#### ONCE A MONTH

**Inspect detergent tray** *If washing powder clogs tray because of insufficient water pressure or using too much detergent, clothes won't be properly cleaned.*

**Clean door glass** *Limescale and other debris can allow water to escape between glass and seal.*

**Test door seal** *If seal feels tacky, it's a sign that it is perishing and needs replacing.*

**Turn hot and cold hose taps off and on again** *A flood can result if either tap seizes in the open position and there's a leak in hoses between taps and inlet valves.*

#### EVERY SIX MONTHS

**Clean lint filter** *This coarse sieve catches bits of fluff, small coins and other objects. If it gets blocked, water can remain in the machine and a leak may occur.*

**Empty catchpot** *Machines with no lint filter have one of these to trap items left in pockets and other debris. If not emptied, their contents can be drawn into the pump.*

**Examine inlet hose connections** *Because these are on the back of machine, a leak from one of them can go undetected, causing damage to floor and machine.*

---

### SAFETY WARNING

DIY repairs to appliances may invalidate your warranty and can be dangerous. Always call an expert if you are in doubt.

## Cleaning the lint filter

Open the access hatch on the front of the machine, undo the filter cap and pull out the filter assembly. Remove fluff and other debris, rinse and refit.

## Cleaning the detergent tray

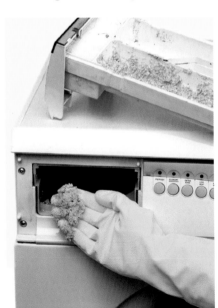

Pull the tray or drawer right out to clean it and examine the recess too; on some machines, this area can also become clogged with detergent.

## Cleaning the glass door

Dip an abrasive pad in clean, warm water, and rub debris off the glass, concentrating on the area that touches the seal.

## Fitting a new handle

**1** Replacement door handle kits are available for most models. To remove the faulty handle, you must first take the door off the machine by undoing the hinges. This often reveals a small cut-out, normally hidden by the hinge, in the door inset.

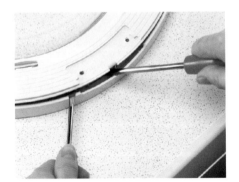

**2** Starting at the cut-out, use two flat-bladed screwdrivers to lever the inset away from the outer rim, stepping one screwdriver over the other until the two parts click apart. With the inset removed, dismantle the handle and fit the new one.

# FAULT DIAGNOSIS

*If your machine starts to leak, the water itself provides a clue as to where the fault lies. If the water is clear without any detergent in it, you know the leak must be occurring before the water reaches the detergent tray. If the water is soapy, the door seal or pump could be leaking. If the water is dirty, the blame may well lie with a defective drain hose or a blockage in the lint filter or the outlet.*

## MACHINE WON'T START

Door not shut properly *Check door and close if necessary.*
Faulty interlock won't allow door to shut *Contact qualified repairer.*
No power *Check flex, plug wiring, fuse and mains supply for faults.*
Faulty on/off switch (check power light if fitted) *Contact qualified repairer.*

## NO WATER ENTERING

Inlet hose kinked *Free trapped hose.*
Taps turned off *Open taps.*
Inlet valve filter blocked *Clean valve filter (page 67).*
Pressure system blocked in pressurised state *This causes appliance to act as if it is full of water. Contact qualified repairer.*

## MACHINE OVERFILLS AND FLOODS

Inlet valve staying open or pressure switch not operating *Disconnect from power supply. If water continues to flow in, hot or cold inlet valve is faulty. Discover which by turning off each tap in turn. Replace valve. If water stops flowing in, pressure system is at fault. Contact qualified repairer.*

## STUCK ON WASH CYCLE

Faulty timer *Move programmer to spin cycle. Contact qualified repairer.*
Faulty heater or thermostat *Contact qualified repairer.*

## DRUM WON'T ROTATE

Loose or worn drive belt *Adjust or replace belt.*
Worn motor brushes *Contact qualified repairer.*
Faulty timer *Contact qualified repairer.*
Faulty spin control unit *Contact qualified repairer.*

## DOOR WON'T OPEN AT THE END OF PROGRAMME

Worn door seal *Old door seals can become sticky with age and adhere to glass. Carefully ease door open, then replace seal (page 70).*
Water still in machine *Repeat spin cycle to operate pump again. Inspect filter and clean if necessary. Inspect outlet hoses for kinks or blockages.*
Door interlock faulty *Contact qualified repairer.*
Door handle broken *Replace handle (opposite).*

## CLOTHES DAMAGED

Water overheating due to faulty programmer *Contact qualified repairer.*
Water overheating due to faulty thermostat *Contact qualified repairer.*
Drum damaged or metal object trapped in machine *Contact qualified repairer.*

## CLOTHES STILL DIRTY

Detergent dispenser clogged *Clean dispenser (opposite).*
Loose or broken drum drive belt *Contact qualified repairer.*
Worn brushes *Contact qualified repairer.*

## Replacing a door seal

**1** Locate the outer clamp band securing the seal to the shell of the machine and examine it carefully. Many can be carefully prised off with a flat-bladed screwdriver, but some have a tensioning arrangement that has to be loosened. After removing the outer clamp band, locate the inner one securing the seal to the drum and establish how this is secured. It may be necessary to loosen a clip, or you may be able to prise the band off with a flat-bladed screwdriver.

**2** Once the clamp bands have been removed, use both hands to pull the seal away from the locating lips on the shell and drum.

Rubbing a smear of fabric conditioner into the groove that locates the seal on the drum makes fitting the new seal easier. If the clamp band has no tensioning adjustment, fit it on the bottom of the seal first, then push the rest of it on with both hands working in opposite directions towards the top.

# Tumble-dryer

A tumble-dryer rotates wet laundry inside a drum while blowing hot air through it to dry it. The faults that arise are similar to those encountered with a washing machine.

Repair and maintenance is easier if you understand how a tumble-dryer works. Once you have placed clean, washed and spun clothes in the dryer's drum you will need to shut the door firmly – the dryer will not start until the door is shut and the door catch engaged. After selecting the temperature, the electric motor is started by turning the timer knob. This powers a drive belt to turn the drum, and directly drives the blower.

After a few revolutions to allow the damp clothes to separate around the drum, the heating element switches on.

A thermostat controls the heating element. Hot air is blown through the rotating clothes, evaporating the moisture.

The air then passes out of the drum through the lint filter to the exhaust vent.

Cold air is drawn in at the top rear of the unit and passes over the drum and motor before being blown by the fan over the heating elements. The hot air then flows through the drum and rotating clothes and out through a filter into a vent pipe. Any obstruction in this flow can inhibit the action of the machine. A cut-out fuse stops the drum from overheating.

As clothes are tumble dried, they drop fibres. Most of this fluff is trapped by the lint filter, which is usually in the door, and this needs to be checked and cleaned regularly. Lint also builds up in the vent pipe and around the electric motor.

## Condenser dryers

Some dryers and those incorporated into combined washer-dryers are condenser dryers. They blow the evaporated moisture from your laundry over a cool surface, causing the moisture to condense to water. This is either collected in a container that must be emptied, or is pumped away through the waste water system.

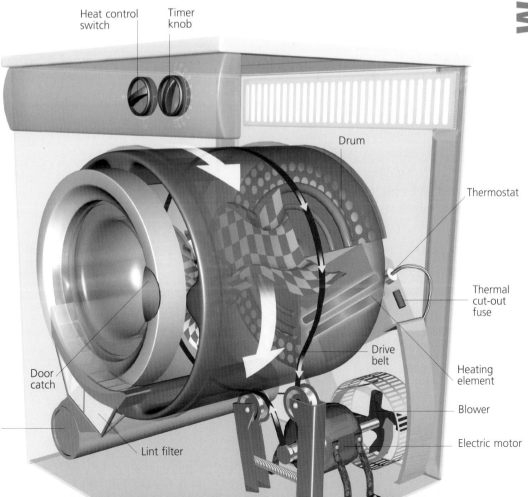

Heat control switch · Timer knob · Drum · Thermostat · Thermal cut-out fuse · Heating element · Drive belt · Blower · Electric motor · Lint filter · Door catch · Exhaust tube to vent at rear

## Cleaning the lint filter

Wait until the dryer cools, open the door and lift out the lint filter. Gently brush off lint using your fingers. On many models, the filter may also be washed. Check your manual for instructions.

## Cleaning inside the dryer

Make sure the dryer is cool, switch it off and unplug it. Unscrew the retaining screws on the back panel, and lift it off. Vacuum the blower area. Also vacuum around the vent pipe connection. Replace the back panel and replace all the screws.

### MAINTENANCE

*Make sure the tumble-dryer is level and does not rock, and consult the manufacturer's instructions for the maximum weight of clothing to dry at one time. Also, make sure clothes have been spun-dry before putting them into the dryer.*

#### AFTER EACH USE

Clean lint filter *Dryer designs vary but the lint filter should lift or slide out easily. Clear the screen (left) and reinstall, seating it properly.*

#### EVERY SIX MONTHS

Vacuum area where lint filter sits *Remove filter and use a narrow vacuum nozzle to remove dust and lint from fitting.*
Vacuum heater area, blower housing and vent pipe connection *Unplug dryer, remove back, making sure you do not catch or dislodge any wires or connections. See below left.*
Check external vent (if fitted) *Make sure there are no obstructions in the vent.*

#### ONCE A YEAR

Remove and check entire vent pipe for lint *Make sure there are no snags or sharp turns on the pipe, which can collect dust or moisture.*

## FAULT DIAGNOSIS

### DRYER WON'T START

No power to appliance *Check mains lead, plug fuse and wiring, and mains supply.*
Door switch faulty *Verify nothing is blocking door catch. If not, contact qualified repairer to replace switch.*
Timer switch faulty *Reset timer and try again. If the symptom persists, contact qualified repairer to replace timer switch.*
Delay timer faulty *If a delay timer is fitted, check that it has not been reset. If the symptom persists, contact a qualified repairer to replace switch.*

### TIMER TURNS BUT DRYER DRUM DOES NOT ROTATE

Drum motor faulty *Contact qualified repairer.*
Drum belt snapped *Contact qualified repairer.*
Timer switch faulty *Reset timer and try again. If the symptom persists, contact qualified repairer to replace switch.*
Reversing timer faulty (if fitted) *Reset timer and try again. If the symptom persists, contact qualified repairer.*

### CLOTHES NOT DRYING BUT DRUM AND TIMER BOTH TURN

Thermostat faulty *Contact qualified repairer.*
Heating element faulty *If there is some heat when a high setting is selected, the element may be faulty. Contact qualified repairer.*
Thermal cut-out fuse has operated *Wait 15 minutes and try again. If the symptom persists, replace thermal fuse if accessible. Refer to manual and replace with manufacturer's recommended thermal fuse. Otherwise, contact qualified repairer.*

### CLOTHES SLOW TO DRY

Heating element faulty *Contact qualified repairer.*
Heat control switch faulty *Contact qualified repairer.*
Restricted air flow *Clean the lint filter and the vent pipe.*
Machine overloaded *Consult manufacturer's instructions for correct loads.*
Over-wet clothes *Make sure clothes are spun dry before placing them in the tumble dryer.*
Thermostat faulty *Contact qualified repairer.*

### CLOTHES OVERHEAT OR BURN

Thermostat faulty *Contact qualified repairer.*
Cut-out faulty *Contact qualified repairer.*

### CLOTHES TANGLED OR CREASED

Reversing timer faulty *Turn machine off and on again. If symptom persists, contact qualified repairer to replace timer.*
Timer switch faulty *Reset timer and try again. If symptom persists, contact qualified repairer.*

### NO DELAY OPERATION (IF FITTED)

Delay timer faulty *Contact qualified repairer.*

### ODOURS

Blocked lint filter *Clean lint filter.*

### NOISY OPERATION

Object in drum *Open and remove.*
Worn bearings *Contact qualified repairer.*

# Fridge-freezer

Refrigerators and freezers work by taking heat from inside the appliance and transferring it to the outside. This is achieved by the repeated evaporation and condensation of a substance called a refrigerant. Keep an eye on the temperature inside the fridge and freezer – if it is too high, your food will not be being stored safely. It is also important to monitor the frost levels in the freezer unit, as frost build-up impairs the freezer's efficiency and it will cost more to run.

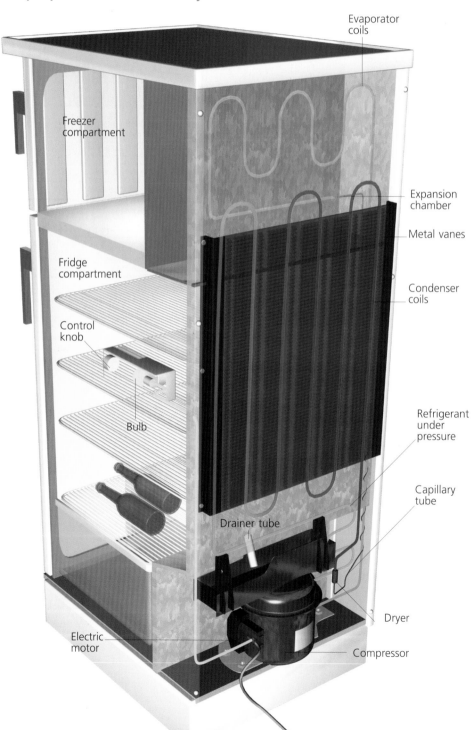

Evaporator coils

Freezer compartment

Expansion chamber

Metal vanes

Fridge compartment

Condenser coils

Control knob

Bulb

Refrigerant under pressure

Capillary tube

Drainer tube

Dryer

Electric motor

Compressor

A fridge and freezer work by using the heat inside the compartments to make the refrigerant evaporate (change from a liquid into a gas). The refrigerant travels outside the compartment and condenses back into a liquid, giving out heat.

An electric motor drives a compressor, which pressurises the refrigerant gas and pumps it round the system through a series of coils at the back of the unit. The condenser coils act as small radiators, giving off heat into the room.

A thermostat connected to the control knob case maintains the temperature by switching the compressor on and off.

## Cleaning the door gasket

Clean the rubber door seal of both the fridge and freezer compartments with detergent solution. Make sure all the dirt is removed from between the grooves. Then rinse and wipe dry.

## Cleaning the back

Gently vacuum around the condenser coils and motor to remove any accumulated dust and dirt.

## Cleaning the fridge interior

Remove glass and plastic shelves and allow them to reach room temperature before washing in warm detergent solution. Rinse and wipe dry. Wash the fridge compartment with a baking soda solution. Use coat-hanger wire to carefully remove food or mould from the drain hole at the back of the compartment.

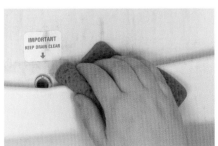

IMPORTANT
KEEP DRAIN CLEAR

---

### MAINTENANCE

#### EVERY 4-6 MONTHS

**Defrost freezer** *Frost build-up reduces freezer efficiency. If there is not an automatic defrost system, turn the thermostat to 'Off' or 'Defrost'. Remove all food from freezer compartment, wrap in newspaper or blankets and store in a cool place. Then unplug appliance and carefully scrape away frost and ice from inside freezer with a plastic tool. When defrosting is complete, clean compartment with baking soda solution, rinse and allow to dry before turning unit back on.*

**Clean interior of fridge** *Remove all food, racks and drawers. Make sure drain hole is clear.*

**Clean door gasket** *Dirt can ruin seal around the door, allowing cool air to escape.*

**Vacuum around back of fridge-freezer** *Be careful near condenser coils.*

---

### MOVING A FRIDGE-FREEZER

Open the door and place one hand inside to lift the front. If possible, place your other hand on a worktop to give you support. Then wiggle the appliance gently from side to side as you pull it forwards. Always allow a fridge-freezer to settle for a couple of hours with the power switched off before and after moving it.

---

### SAFETY WARNING

Always unplug, disconnect or isolate any appliance when carrying out cleaning or maintenance.

## Checking the thermostat

Refrigerators keep food at temperatures that slow down the growth of bacteria. Freezers stop bacterial activity altogether. If a fridge-freezer is not maintained properly and its temperature closely monitored, bacteria can breed.

**1** Set the thermostat to its lowest setting (usually called '1'). Put a glass of water in the centre of the fridge for 24 hours, then check its temperature with a fridge thermometer. The temperature should be between 0°C and 5°C.

**2** If the temperature is not within the safe range, make sure the thermostat sensor (a small metal tube with a thin tube running to the thermostat) is not covered with anything – spilt food for example.
If it is clean, the thermostat may be faulty, so contact a qualified repairer.

### SAFETY WARNING

DIY repairs to appliances may invalidate your warranty and can be dangerous. Always call an expert if you are in doubt.

### FAULT DIAGNOSIS

#### FRIDGE TOO COLD OR TOO WARM

Thermostat tube blocked or covered *Check thermostat accuracy.*
Thermostat control loose *Check and replace control knob.*
Frost build-up *Defrost fridge.*
Door seal ineffective *Check seal is clean and has no tears in it. Clean or replace if possible.*
Faulty thermostat *Contact qualified repairer.*

#### FRIDGE-FREEZER NOT WORKING BUT LIGHT ON

Thermostat off or set to 'defrost' *Adjust to normal setting.*
Faulty thermostat *Contact qualified repairer.*
Faulty compressor *Contact qualified repairer.*

#### LIGHT NOT WORKING

Bulb blown *Replace with correct type and wattage.*
Door switch faulty *Clean away any dirt around switch. If it still doesn't work, contact qualified repairer.*

#### COMPRESSOR MOTOR RUNS CONTINUOUSLY

Faulty thermostat *Contact qualified repairer.*
Loss of refrigerant *Contact qualified repairer.*
Faulty compressor *Contact qualified repairer.*

#### FREEZER OFTEN NEEDS DEFROSTING

Faulty door seal *Clean or replace if possible.*

#### WATER ACCUMULATES IN THE BASE OF THE FRIDGE

Blocked drainer tube *Drainer tube is small rubber cylinder in the back wall of the fridge. Remove debris taking care not to puncture tube.*

# Dishwasher

**A dishwasher uses two rotating arms to spray water and detergent over dishes and utensils before pumping away the dirty water and rinsing the dishes clean. Many problems can be avoided by keeping the machine clean.**

Dishwashers save time on washing up, although they are costly in terms of electricity since the water is heated to very high temperatures. Detergent is placed in the soap dispenser. A timer mechanism sets the washing programme.

The washer starts as soon as the door is closed and will stop at any point in the washing cycle if the door is opened. Hot water enters through the inlet valve and passes through a water softener to the sump. Here it mixes with the detergent, which has been released into the machine.

An electric pump draws the water through a strainer, over a heating element and supplies it to the sprayer arms. A thermostat controls the element to maintain the correct washing temperature.

The water sprays from angled nozzles in the sprayer arms, turning them in the same way as a garden sprinkler. When the wash cycle ends, the dirty water is pumped away from the sump.

The timer activates a cool or cold rinse and then a second heated rinse. The hot rinsing water is pumped away leaving very hot dishes that dry quickly.

## SAFETY WARNING

DIY repairs to appliances may invalidate your warranty and can be dangerous. Always call an expert if you are in doubt.

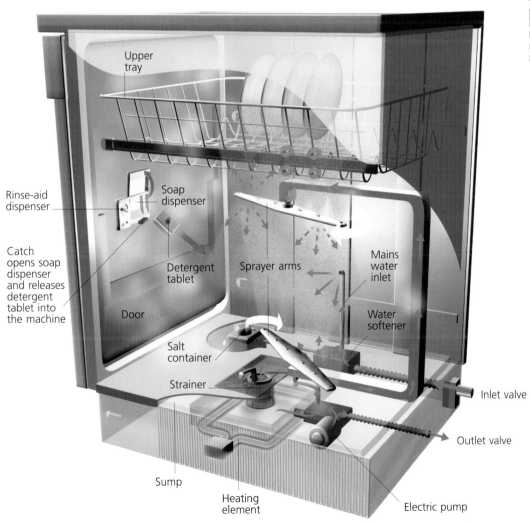

Upper tray

Rinse-aid dispenser

Soap dispenser

Catch opens soap dispenser and releases detergent tablet into the machine

Detergent tablet

Sprayer arms

Mains water inlet

Door

Water softener

Salt container

Strainer

Inlet valve

Outlet valve

Sump

Heating element

Electric pump

## MAINTENANCE

### EVERY WEEK

Remove, clean and rinse main strainer *There may be a secondary filter inside.*
Check sprayer arms for blocked holes *Clean if blocked.*
Check sprayer arms rotate freely *If not, remove and clean pivot.*
Check rinse-aid level *Refer to small glass window on rinse-aid dispenser inside door. Top up when required.*
Check salt levels *Undo cap and check level if your dishwasher has no warning light.*

### EVERY SIX MONTHS

Check and clean door seal *Use non-abrasive detergent.*
Check condition of hoses *Clean out any deposits from hoses and inlet filter.*
Run cleaning programme using proprietary cleaner *Follow manufacturer's instructions and rinse through after cleaning.*

## SAFETY WARNING

Be careful when you open the door of a dishwasher – very hot steam can escape from the interior of the machine when it is first opened at the end of a cycle.

If you open the door while the wash cycle is still in progress, scalding hot water may spray out. Always pull the door just slightly ajar and wait for a few moments for the water to subside before opening the door fully.

## SAFETY WARNING

Always unplug, disconnect or isolate any appliance when carrying out cleaning or maintenance.

## Cleaning the main strainer

Remove lower basket. Unscrew retaining screws, if any, and lift out filter. Some dishwashers may have two-part filters (above). Wash under running water using household detergent. Rinse thoroughly and then refit.

## Cleaning the sprayer arms

The sprayer arms are held in place either by a simple clip or a locking nut. Remove each sprayer arm separately to clean. Rinse through under the tap and make sure no flakes of limescale or food are blocking the holes. Use a toothpick to clear the sprayer holes of debris if necessary.

## Correctly loading the dishwasher

Loading your dishwasher correctly and using the correct detergent and rinse-aid can help to prolong the operating life of the machine. It is also essential to use the correct type of salt to keep the water softener working properly, unless your house has softened water already. This, in turn, ensures that there is no harmful build-up of limescale within the dishwasher.

When you are loading the dishwasher, make sure that nothing protrudes from the racks – this will stop them running freely as you slide them back into the machine. Any items that can stop the sprayer arms turning freely, such as saucepan handles and knives (below top) will prevent the machine from washing properly. You should also be careful to ensure that no item will stop the soap dispenser opening once the door is closed.

**Avoid sticky glasses** Using too much rinse aid in the machine can leave glasses stickier than when they went into the dishwasher. Check the operating manual and adjust the quantity of rinse aid as necessary.

### FAULT DIAGNOSIS

#### MACHINE DOES NOT FUNCTION

No power to dishwasher *Check flex, plug wiring, fuse, and mains supply for faults.*
Door switch not closed *Check loading of items and that door is properly closed.*
No water *Ensure water supply is present and turned on. Check for hose filter blockages.*

#### NO WATER PRESENT

No water supply *Ensure water supply is present and turned on.*
Inlet valve blocked or faulty *Check for blockages. Test the valve's operation with a multimeter. Replace valve if necessary.*

#### DOES NOT WASH CLEAN

Incorrect quantities of detergent *Refer to manual.*
Machine incorrectly loaded *Refer to manual.*
Sump filter blocked *Clean filter.*

#### DOES NOT EMPTY

Sump strainer or filter blocked *Clean filter.*
Blocked sump or drain hose *Check and clear.*
Faulty drain pump motor *Consult qualified repairer.*

#### WHITE STREAKS ON DISHES

No (or insufficient) salt *Check salt dispenser (see manual).*
Machine not rinsing properly *Consult qualified repairer.*
Softener unit faulty *Consult qualified repairer.*

#### RING MARKS ON GLASS ITEMS

Too little rinse-aid *Check level and setting (see manual). Top up if necessary.*

# Ovens and hobs

The main maintenance task for an oven is to keep it as clean as possible. Otherwise, a build-up of spills and grease can cause smoke and fumes. Hobs require cleaning after every use.

## Cleaning the oven walls

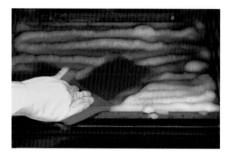

Spray a proprietary oven cleaner inside your oven and leave it to work for the time specified in the manufacturer's instructions. Then use a clean sponge to wipe off the foam residue. Wear rubber gloves to prevent the cleaner coming into contact with your skin and make sure the kitchen is well ventilated to disperse the fumes from the cleaner. Repeat if necessary.

## Cleaning the oven door

If possible, remove the oven door glass, or the whole door, following the manufacturer's instructions. Use warm water with a little detergent to clean the glass sections of the door. Use a mild abrasive cleaner for burned-on dirt.

## Cleaning a gas hob

Lift off the pan supports and wash in warm, soapy water. Use a cloth soaked in warm water, with a little cream cleaner to remove caked-on food and wash the surface of the cooker, taking care not to get water into the burners. Remove burner caps, wipe and replace them and the pan supports. Turn the burners on for a short while to evaporate any excess water.

## Changing the door gasket

Turn off the oven at the mains supply and allow it to cool. Open the oven door and carefully peel away the worn rubber gasket from the door frame. Then press in the replacement gasket.

## FAULT DIAGNOSIS

### NO FUNCTIONS

No power *Check wall switch is on and MCB in consumer unit has not tripped off. If it has, reset it to 'on'. If you cannot, call an electrician to trace and rectify the fault.*

### ELECTRIC ELEMENT(S) NOT WORKING

Thermostat tripped *Turn off oven and wait until it has fully cooled down before trying again.*
Timer set to Auto *Make sure timer is set to Manual.*
Element failed *Contact qualified repairer.*
Control thermostat faulty *Contact qualified repairer.*

### OVEN NOT COOKING EVENLY

Faulty or jammed fan *Check and clean. Consult qualified repairer.*
Incorrect shelf positions *Make sure temperatures and shelf positions are correct.*

### DOOR WON'T CLOSE

Hinge spring or latch defective *Replace, following manufacturer's instructions.*
Gasket worn *Replace door gasket – the rubber or plastic seal on interior door edge or on body of cooker.*

### NO LIGHT

Bulb blown *For many ovens, it is possible to change bulb from inside oven compartment. If this isn't possible, change the bulb by removing the back of the oven. Follow manufacturer's instructions.*

### SPARKS OR BURNING SMELL

Loose connections or poor contacts *Turn off immediately and contact qualified repairer.*

## MICROWAVE OVENS

Microwaves use high-frequency radio waves to heat food. Leaks of such waves are damaging and can be hard to detect. If the door does not close properly or the door seals appear loose, do not use the machine and contact a qualified repairer. Because of the high voltage inside, you should never remove the main cover of a microwave oven and you should refer all faults to a qualified repairer. Nevertheless, you can ensure a long service from your machine through regular cleaning.

**1** Use a non-abrasive cleaning product to remove dirt from the cooking chamber. Make sure the door seal, control panel and exterior panels are clean. Check that nothing is clogging the ventilation slots, either under or on top of the unit.

**2** Remove the turntable and wash it with warm water and washing-up liquid. Clean the rotating ring (or spider) and turntable area thoroughly.

## SAFETY WARNING

DIY repairs to appliances may invalidate your warranty and can be dangerous. Always call an expert if you are in doubt.

# Cooker hood

A cooker hood removes cooking odours and droplets of grease from the air above a hob using a fan and a filter. Regular cleaning is important to avoid a build-up of grease. If grease builds up on the internal fan, it will impair the hood's efficiency.

A cooker hood switch turns on the fan and controls its speed. Another switch turns the light on and off. On some models the fan and light are switched on automatically when the front panel is opened.

The fan draws air from above the hob through a grease filter. In recirculating hoods, an activated charcoal filter removes smells before the air is passed back into the kitchen. These filters must be disposed of and replaced every six months.

If the hood is the type that vents the air to the outside, the grease filter will be thicker. The air is pumped through a pipe leading to a vent in the wall. In these hoods the filter can be cleaned and put back.

## MAINTENANCE

### ONCE A MONTH

Clean grease filter *If cooker hood only vents air, then soak the grease filter, which looks like a screen, in a degreasing agent, followed by warm soapy water.*
Clean interior and exterior of hood *Turn off power at local socket outlet or fused connection unit and clean with a non-abrasive cleaner. Avoid getting liquid in lamp socket.*

### EVERY SIX MONTHS

Change grease and charcoal filters *If cooker hood is recirculating type, replace both grease and charcoal filters. Always use recommended parts for your particular model.*

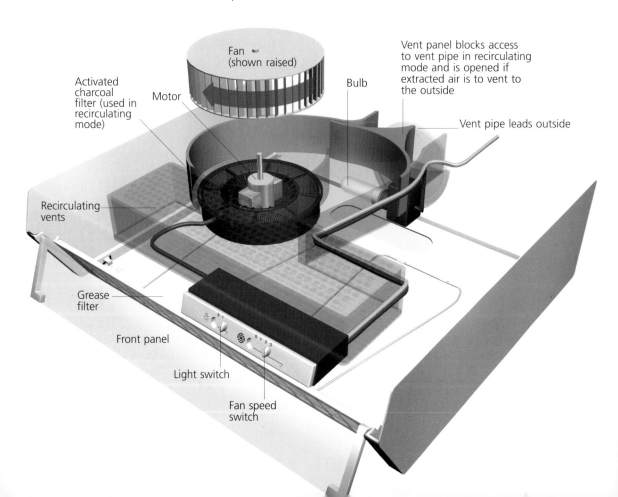

Fan (shown raised)

Activated charcoal filter (used in recirculating mode)

Motor

Bulb

Vent panel blocks access to vent pipe in recirculating mode and is opened if extracted air is to vent to the outside

Vent pipe leads outside

Recirculating vents

Grease filter

Front panel

Light switch

Fan speed switch

## Cleaning the filter

Remove the filter by pressing the release switches and lowering the panel. Unclip the filter and soak it in a degreasing agent, then clean with warm soapy water. If you have a dishwasher, wash the filter in the upper rack.

## Cleaning the fan

**1** Switch off the cooker hood and turn off the power at the local socket outlet or fused connection unit. Unclip the activated charcoal filter, if fitted, and remove it.

**2** Locate the circular motor and fan unit beneath the charcoal filter. Remove the fan mounting screws. Then carefully slide out the motor unit and fan assembly.

**3** Unscrew the central retaining screw and remove the fan blades. Soak in warm water and washing-up liquid or a degreasing agent. Clean and dry, then refit.

### FAULT DIAGNOSIS

#### LIGHT WORKS BUT FAN DOES NOT TURN

Fan switch faulty *Contact qualified repairer.*
Motor burnt out *Contact qualified repairer.*
Jammed fan blades *Remove fan blades and clean with degreasing agent or washing-up liquid.*

#### LIGHT DOES NOT WORK

Bulb blown *Turn off power at fused connection unit, or disconnect hood from mains supply. Then open hood and replace bulb.*
Faulty switch or wiring *Contact qualified repairer.*

#### NOTHING WORKS

No power *Check for blown fuse in plug or fused connection unit, or tripped circuit breaker in consumer unit.*

#### FAN NOISY

Greasy fan blades *Remove fan blades and clean with degreasing agent or washing-up liquid.*
Blocked filters *Clean or replace.*
Worn motor or fan bearings *Lubricate with light oil, or call qualified repairer.*

### SAFETY WARNING

Always unplug, disconnect or isolate any appliance when carrying out cleaning or maintenance.

## Replacing the filters

If the cooker hood recycles air, the filters cannot be cleaned. Replace both the grease filter and the activated charcoal filter every six months, depending on usage.

# Food processor

**Using interchangeable metal and plastic tools, a food processor can chop, slice, shred, grate and mix a wide range of foodstuffs. Cleaning your processor thoroughly after every use is the best way to keep it in good working order.**

Food processors come with a range of blades, each suited to a specific task or tasks. The blade is slotted onto the spindle, or, in the case of graters and chippers, is mounted on an extension spindle so as to cut just under the fill tube.

Plastic nibs and other small parts, where the lid of the mixer compartment twists and locks into place or where the plunger pushes down into the fill tube, are liable to break over time. Bowls also often crack or get broken. Making a hygienic repair is impossible, but replacement parts are available for most models.

Through use, the blades will gradually become blunt. As with all blades, it is better to sharpen them a little and often than to attempt to restore them once they are completely blunt.

Some models come with a liquidiser and blunt plastic blades for kneading dough.

## MAINTENANCE

### AFTER EACH USE

Clean blades and bowl *Wash up by hand or clean by running the machine with hot soapy water inside (see opposite).*
Clean case *See opposite.*

### AS REQUIRED

Sharpen cutter blades *See opposite.*

## SAFETY WARNING

DIY repairs to appliances may invalidate your warranty and may be dangerous. Call an expert if you are in doubt.

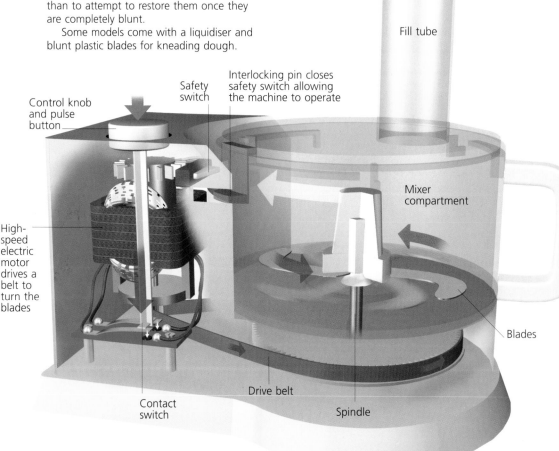

Fill tube

Safety switch

Interlocking pin closes safety switch allowing the machine to operate

Control knob and pulse button

Mixer compartment

High-speed electric motor drives a belt to turn the blades

Blades

Contact switch

Drive belt

Spindle

## Cleaning the bowl

Fill the bowl half full of hot water with a little washing-up liquid, then run the processor at top speed. Make sure the spindle and inside of any plastic parts are clean. Rinse and dry.

The chopping blades of a liquidiser cannot be removed, so this is also a good method for cleaning them.

## Cleaning the case

Clean case with a mild detergent, keeping away from vents. Remove debris from vents with a soft brush.

## Sharpening the blades

Push the edge of the blade away from you along a wet sharpening stone (available from DIY shops). Repeat the process for each blade which needs to be sharpened.

### FAULT DIAGNOSIS

#### NO FUNCTIONS

No power *Check flex, plug wiring, fuse and mains supply for faults.*
Safety switch not closed *Check that lid is fitted correctly and that interlock pin on the lid engages safety switch.*
Thermal cut-out tripped *Wait a few moments to see if it resets. If it cuts out again, make sure you have not overfilled processor.*
Motor burned out *Contact qualified engineer.*

#### BOWL LEAKS

Bowl overfull *Do not fill bowl above specified maximum line.*
Bowl cracked *Buy new bowl.*

#### SOLID FOOD STICKS ON BLADES

Blades blunt *Sharpen cutter blades.*
Chunks of food too large *Cut food into smaller pieces before filling.*
Wrong cutting option *Use push button pulse mode.*

#### BLADES NOT TURNING BUT MOTOR RUNNING

Broken or worn drive belt *Take machine to professional repairer to fit new drive belt.*

### SAFETY WARNING

Food processor blades are extremely sharp. Always handle them with care when washing or sharpening them.

# Electric kettle

Regular cleaning and descaling will help to prevent breakdowns and keep your kettle on the boil.

## Washing the filter

Remove the lid and rinse out the kettle. Slide out the filter and wash away any limescale. Clean the filter using a soft brush and washing-up liquid. Rinse the filter well.

## Cleaning steam vents

Make sure the kettle is cold and open the lid. Use a toothpick to gently scrape away any flakes of limescale blocking the steam vent at the rear. Also check exterior vents for dirt or debris.

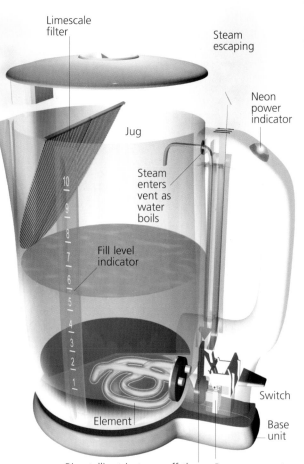

Limescale filter

Steam escaping

Neon power indicator

Jug

Steam enters vent as water boils

Fill level indicator

Switch

Element

Base unit

Bimetallic strip turns off the element when heated by escaping steam

Power connector between base unit and jug

| FAULT DIAGNOSIS |
| --- |
| **WATER DOES NOT HEAT UP** |
| No power *Check wiring in plug and fuse for faults.*<br>Faulty element *Replace kettle.*<br>Switch faulty *Replace kettle.* |
| **SLOW TO REACH BOIL** |
| Limescale build-up on element *Descale kettle.* |
| **BOILS FOR A LONG TIME** |
| Blocked steam vents *Clean steam vents.* |

| MAINTENANCE |
| --- |
| **AS REQUIRED** |
| Descale kettle *Limescale build-up can reduce efficiency and lead to failure of the element. You will need to descale kettles more often in hard-water areas than soft.*<br>Wash filter *Kettle must be cold.* |

| SAFETY WARNING |
| --- |
| DIY repairs to appliances may invalidate your warranty and may be dangerous. Call an expert if you are in doubt. |

# Iron

Dirt and limescale from hard water are the biggest enemies of a steam iron. Over time, repeated use and movement may cause the flex to fray.

Once the iron is plugged in, a heating element warms the soleplate to a temperature determined by a control knob and an adjustable thermostat. A thermal fuse cuts the power if the iron overheats. Some irons have a mercury switch to turn the element off if the iron is left in the horizontal position for too long.

## Cleaning an iron

**1** Gently clear steam vents with a pipe cleaner or toothpick.

**2** Use a very fine sewing needle to clean the spray nozzle. Be careful not to enlarge the opening by pressing too hard.

**3** Flush the iron out with a proprietary cleaning product. Place the iron on a metal rack over a large pan and set to steam until the tank is empty. Repeat with clean water.

| FAULT DIAGNOSIS |
| --- |
| **IRON DOESN'T HEAT** |
| No power *Check flex, wiring, fuse and mains supply for faults.* Control knob set at cold *Adjust.* |
| **NO STEAM** |
| Not enough water in reservoir *Wrong steam valve or thermostat setting. Adjust.* Steam valve blocked *Activate steam button a few times to clear.* |
| **SOLEPLATE LEAKS WATER** |
| Soleplate not hot enough *Increase setting.* Variable steam control set too high *Reduce setting.* Bursts of steam too frequent *Allow more time between bursts.* |
| **IRON STICKS TO OR STAINS FABRIC** |
| Burned material stuck to soleplate *Clean soleplate.* |

| MAINTENANCE |
| --- |
| **AFTER EACH USE** |
| Clean the soleplate with a damp cloth while still warm *Do not use an abrasive cleaner.* Empty residual water according to manufacturer's instructions |
| **ONCE A MONTH OR AS ADVISED** |
| Clean out iron *Follow the manufacturer's instructions.* Check for damaged flex *Get frayed flex replaced by a professional if necessary.* |
| **AS ADVISED** |
| Descale iron *Follow the manufacturer's instructions.* |

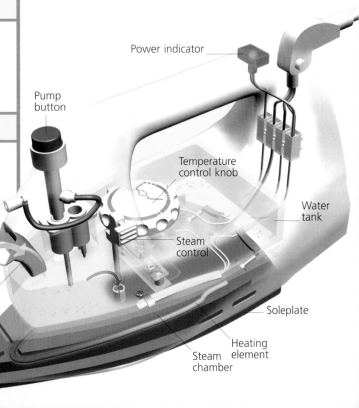

Power indicator

Pump button

Temperature control knob

Water tank

Steam control

Soleplate

Heating element

Steam chamber

Water is poured in through the spout and drips into the steam chamber

# Filter coffeemaker

Water runs through narrow tubes to be heated and these are prone to furring up with limescale. Descale it often and look out for chips in the glass carafe, and your coffeemaker will serve you well for many years.

## MAINTENANCE

### AS REQUIRED

Flush mineral deposits from the system using commercial descaler *Limescale builds up rapidly in small tubes, especially if you live in a hard-water area.*

### ONCE A MONTH

Check carafe for cracks and chips *Replace it if you find any damage; it could leak or break when heated.*

## FAULT DIAGNOSIS

### NO HEAT

Faulty element *Check and replace or buy a new machine.*
No power *Lead damaged or on/off switch faulty. Switch off coffeemaker and unplug from mains supply. Remove retaining screw from plug to check plug wiring and fuse.*

### WEAK COFFEE

Drip holes blocked *Empty coffeemaker, remove carafe, and unclog holes using a toothpick.*

### LITTLE OR NO HOT WATER FROM DRIP HEAD

One-way valve clogged or jammed *Clean valve unit or replace.* Tubes blocked with mineral deposits *Flush out using a descaler.* Drip holes blocked *See above.*

Cold water flows from the reservoir down through a one-way valve into a curved aluminium tube attached to a heating element in the base of the machine. The water rises as it is heated and is discharged from the drip head to percolate through the ground coffee into the glass carafe.

   The most common problems are for the one-way valve, tubes or drip head to become blocked, or for the glass carafe to get damaged. The heating element may also fail. It is possible to repair or replace parts, but it may be more cost effective to replace the machine.

Mesh filter

Drip head

Case with water reservoir

Ground coffee

Riser tube

One-way valve

Glass carafe

Heating element

Switch

Thermostat

Tube connectors

Aluminium tube

Metal plate

# Toaster

Modern toasters rely increasingly on electronic rather than mechanical controllers. This means there are fewer maintenance and repair tasks that you can perform yourself.

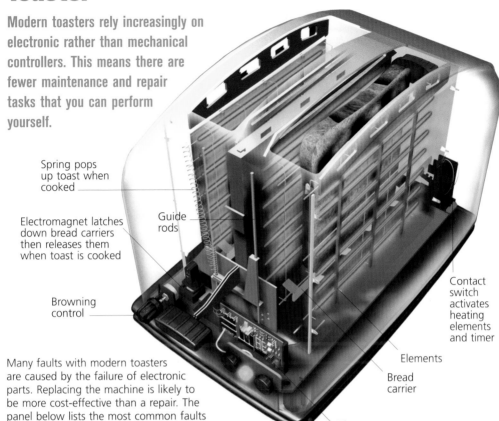

Spring pops up toast when cooked

Electromagnet latches down bread carriers then releases them when toast is cooked

Guide rods

Browning control

Contact switch activates heating elements and timer

Elements

Bread carrier

Timer

Many faults with modern toasters are caused by the failure of electronic parts. Replacing the machine is likely to be more cost-effective than a repair. The panel below lists the most common faults that can be resolved at home.

## MAINTENANCE

### EVERY WEEK

Clean out crumb tray *This usually pulls out from underneath toaster.*

### WHENEVER REQUIRED

Dislodge trapped pieces of bread with non-metallic object *Unplug toaster and wait for it to cool before attempting this. Take great care not to touch heating element wires, which are fragile and easily broken. In stubborn cases, it may be necessary to remove casing to complete job without damaging appliance.*

## FAULT DIAGNOSIS

### CARRIER DOES NOT POP UP

Bread trapped *Turn off toaster and free bread (see maintenance).*

### CARRIER WILL NOT LATCH DOWN

No power to electromagnet *Check mains supply, plug fuse and wiring for faults.*

## SAFETY WARNING

Always unplug, disconnect or isolate any appliance when carrying out cleaning or maintenance.

# Vacuum cleaner

There are three varieties of vacuum cleaner: pull-along cylinder cleaners, push-along uprights and a variant that combines both cylinder and upright into one – often referred to as a hybrid cleaner. All three are available with either dust bags or cyclone bagless filtration systems.

Different cleaners are suited to different tasks, so choosing the right cleaner for your individual circumstances is important. Uprights with belt-driven brush rolls are best for removing pet hair from carpets, while cylinder models are better suited to hard flooring, for example.

Whatever your model, keeping a vacuum cleaner free from blockages can help to avoid expensive repair bills. Replace or empty a dustbag before it is full and check the filters regularly.

## Upright cleaner

In a simple upright cleaner (right), the motor drives both the suction fan and a rubber belt to drive the rotating brush roll, or beater, which loosens dust and dirt from the carpet. Dirty air is drawn over the fan and into the dust bag, where the dust is trapped. The air passes through the twin surfaces of the bag, which act as a filter.

## Cylinder cleaner

In a cylinder cleaner (below right) the motor drives a suction fan, which draws air into the dust bag. Unless a turbo-driven head attachment is used, suction is the only method of drawing dirt out of the carpet. The air is then drawn through a primary filter before reaching the fan, which blows the air out of the cleaner through a HEPA (High Efficiency Particulate Arresting) filter. This filters out the tiniest dust particles.

## Hybrid cleaner

A hybrid cleaner looks like a conventional upright machine, but combines the carpet-beating power of an upright cleaner with a brush roll with the improved filtration of a cylinder model, including a HEPA exhaust filter.

Dust bag acts as a filter for air leaving the machine

Dirty air is sucked into the bag by a suction fan

Brush roll

Suction fan

Electric motor

Cooling fan

Rubber belt drives the brush roll

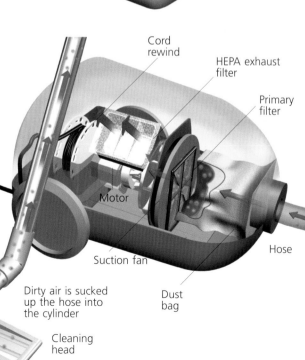

Cord rewind

HEPA exhaust filter

Primary filter

Motor

Suction fan

Hose

Dust bag

Dirty air is sucked up the hose into the cylinder

Cleaning head

## MAINTENANCE

### EVERY THREE MONTHS

Test bag full indicator *Put hand over end of hose to reduce air pressure and simulate 'bag full' conditions.*
Check hose for blockages *Unscrew and examine ends of tubing for fluff obstructions. Drop coin through hose to locate internal blockages.*
Clean brush roll on upright cleaners *Also, check for threads or hair wrapped around shaft or belt and remove by cutting carefully.*

### EVERY SIX MONTHS

Change filters and bag on 'through flow' systems *Over time, filters get blocked and this reduces vacuum cleaner efficiency and can cause the motor to overheat.*
Wash filters on a cyclonic cleaner

### EVERY SIX BAG CHANGES

Replace exhaust filters *If cleaner has a HEPA (High Efficiency Particulate Arresting) exhaust filter, change it regularly.*

## SAFETY WARNING

DIY repairs to appliances may invalidate your warranty and may be dangerous. Always call an expert if you are in doubt.

## Bagless cleaning

Variations of the 'bagless' cyclone system originally developed by James Dyson are now used by many other manufacturers on all different types of cleaner. Bagless cyclone vacuum cleaners filter dirt out of the air by using centrifugal force rather than a dust bag.

Dirty air is drawn by a fan into the top corner of a drum. The angle at which the air enters causes it to spiral round the drum. This creates centrifugal forces that cause the larger dust particles (shown in red on artwork, right) to spin out of the air stream and fall to the bottom of the drum. The air then flows through a filter (which catches more dust particles) and into a conical cylinder, which is housed within the drum.

The angle at which the air enters and the sloping walls of the cylinder combine to cause the air, containing the smallest dust particles (shown in blue), to spin down to the bottom of the cone at an increasing speed. Centrifugal forces acting on the air stream increase, forcing the dust particles against the sides of the cone and through the hole in the bottom of the cone, while the air escapes up the centre.

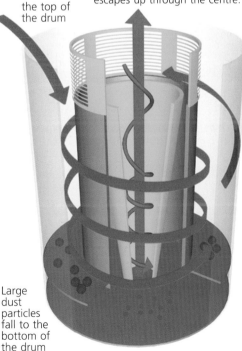

Dirty air enters at the top of the drum

Centrifugal forces send small dust particles (in blue) to the base of the cone, while air escapes up through the centre.

Air passes through a filter into a cone

Large dust particles fall to the bottom of the drum

APPLIANCES

## Changing the filters and bag in a cylinder cleaner

**1** Turn off the cleaner and unplug it. Then open the HEPA filter compartment and replace the filter. You may have to undo a retaining screw.

**2** Replace the primary filter with a new one. If the filters were badly clogged, check the tubes and ducts leading to the bag for blockages.

**3** Replace the bag with the correct type for your model. Make sure it is clipped in place properly and that the hose fits snugly when the lid closes.

## Washing the filter on a bagless cyclonic cleaner

**1** Unplug the vacuum cleaner. Then unclip and open the filter cover, and carefully lift out the circular filter container.

**2** Grip the tab and lift out the foam filter from the container. Wash with a mild detergent then rinse and dry it thoroughly before replacing it in the machine.

## LISTEN FOR WARNING SIGNS

Upright cleaners that use a fan to create the airflow can suffer from damage to the fan, since dirt and debris pass directly from the floor over the fan. Avoid vacuuming hard objects, which could cause problems. If the cleaner is labouring or making an unusual noise, switch it off and unplug it immediately, then check the bag, filters and tube for blockages.

## Replacing the drive belt on an upright cleaner

**1** Turn off and unplug the vacuum cleaner. Remove the front panel or base cover to give access to the motor spindle (this may unclip or have retaining screws).

**2** Remove the worn or broken belt by lifting out the brush roll. Clean the brush roll and bearings then fit the new belt over the motor pulley and then the brush roll and ease the brush roll back into position. Replace the casing.

**Note** Some makes of cleaner use two belts, often of different sizes: it is best to renew both even if only one is broken or worn.

## FAULT DIAGNOSIS

### NO FUNCTIONS

No power to appliance *Check flex, plug fuse and wiring, and mains supply for faults.*
Flex worn *Make sure vacuum cleaner flex is not damaged. Replace if it is.*

### BRUSH ROLLER NOT TURNING

Wrong setting *Check that brush is in carpet mode.*
Wrong brush height *Change setting.*
Hair or threads wrapped around brush *Use a comb to remove hair and lint from brush. Use a sharp knife to cut threads and hairs wrapped around the shaft.*
Broken drive belt *Replace drive belt with the correct part, and check for obstructions.*

### POOR OR NO SUCTION

Bag full *Replace bag.*
Blocked pipes *Check all tubes for obstructions. Remove as necessary.*
Clogged filters *Check and replace. (See manufacturer's manual for specific details.)*
Leaky hose *Check and replace.*

### FLEX WON'T REWIND

Flex tangled *Pull out all the way and untangle flex.*
Spring broken *Contact qualified repairer.*

### NOISY OPERATION

Faulty drive belt *Replace drive belt.*
Motor dirty *Contact qualified repairer.*
Fan broken *Contact qualified repairer.*
Obstruction *Check fan area, tubes and ducts for clogging. Clean if necessary.*

# Electric heaters

A portable electric heater employs a basic fan to blow air over heating elements and out into the room; larger radiant heaters give off heat from glowing bars. Both types need to be kept free from dust, which can ignite when hot.

When a fan heater is turned on, power is supplied to the heating elements and the fan motor. The motor turns the fan blades, drawing air through an air inlet grille in the housing and blowing it over the heating elements and out of the air outlet grille. The degree of warming is controlled by a heat level knob, which varies the amount of current supplied to the elements. A thermostat turns the heater on and off to maintain the required temperature in the room. The air near the motor is not heated and keeps the motor cool.

A radiant heater reflects heat from its bar elements out into a room with the help of a shiny backing plate. It is important to keep the bars and reflective plate clean to ensure that it operates efficiently.

## COOLER CERAMIC

Some fan heaters use ceramic elements. These can operate at lower temperatures while still producing ample heat, and are therefore safer because they do not get as hot.

## MAINTENANCE

*Before attempting any maintenance or repair on an electric heater, switch off the appliance, unplug it and allow it to cool for half an hour.*

### EVERY SIX MONTHS

Clean radiant heater reflectors *Dust or dirt on reflector affects efficiency, and poses a fire risk.* Clean any vents and filters *Make sure dust does not accumulate around air intake and outlet. Keep possible obstructions well clear.* Lubricate motor of fan heater *Apply a drop of light machine oil to motor spindle and bearings as recommended by manufacturer.*

Thermostat control knob

Heat level knob and on/off switch

Air inlet grille

Fan blades

Fan motor

Air outlet grille

Heating elements

## SAFETY WARNING

If incorrectly used, electric heaters can be a fire hazard. As well as keeping the heater free of dust, you must be careful not to cover either the inlet or outlet grille of the heater, or position the heater too close to any flammable items such as curtains or bedspreads. Avoid plugging the heater into a mains multi-plug adaptor.

## Cleaning radiant heaters

**1** Unplug the heater and allow it to cool down. Unscrew and take off the protective metal grille. Remove any dust from the heater elements with a clean soft brush.

**2** Clean both the grille and the reflective plate with a non-flammable metal polish – do not spray it directly onto the elements and make sure no polish residue is left anywhere on the heater. Carefully reassemble the grille and heater, and tighten the retaining screws.

## FAULT DIAGNOSIS

### NO HEAT, FAN NOT TURNING

No power to appliance *Check flex, plug wiring, fuse and mains supply for faults.*
Faulty control switches *Contact qualified repairer.*
Faulty thermostat *Contact qualified repairer.*
Loose connections *Open casing and check connections are secure.*

### NO HEAT, FAN TURNING

Controls set for 'Cold Air' *Adjust.*
Heating element faulty *Contact qualified repairer.*
Faulty control switches *Contact qualified repairer.*
Thermostat tripped *Reset if possible, or allow fan to cool.*

### HEAT FOR SHORT PERIOD, FAN NOT TURNING

Fan blades obstructed *Clean fan blades and remove obstruction.*
Faulty fan motor *Contact qualified repairer.*

### LOW HEAT

Faulty control switches *Contact qualified repairer.*
Faulty thermostat *Contact qualified repairer.*
One or more heating elements broken *Contact qualified repairer.*

### FAN NOISY AND RUNNING SLOW

Motor bearings dry *Open casing and apply lubricating oil to all moving parts.*
Dust and dirt on bearings or blades *Clean interior.*

### BURNING SMELL

Dirty elements, grille and reflector on radiant heater *Clean (see left).*
Dust on element *Clean interior.*

# Extractor fan

Installed in kitchens for removing cooking smells, or in bathrooms and utility rooms to expel moist air, extractor fans are simple devices that create an airflow to the outside.

When the cord switch is pulled, electricity is supplied to the motor inside the unit. In some bathroom versions, power to the fan is controlled by the light switch: when the light switch is pulled or turned on, a power line from the switch turns on the fan. The fan has its own power supply and turns off after a period determined by a timer, set with a trimmer screw (opposite).

The airflow created through the vent as the motor turns the fan causes internal shutters to open. Air flows from the room and out through the outside grille.

Extractor fans need very little maintenance beyond regular cleaning and have few parts that can go wrong. When the motor eventually wears out, replace the entire unit – this will be cheaper than making a repair.

## SAFETY WARNING

With all electrical devices that work near water, such as heated towel rails and extractor fans in bathrooms, installation must comply with electrical safety rules. All appliances must be wired via an unswitched FCU (fused connection unit), which in turn is connected to a ceiling switch inside the bathroom.

## MAINTENANCE

### ONCE A WEEK

Kitchen fan *Wipe blades and vents to remove grease and dust build-up.*

### ONCE A MONTH

Bathroom fan *Clean blades and vents to prevent mould build-up.*

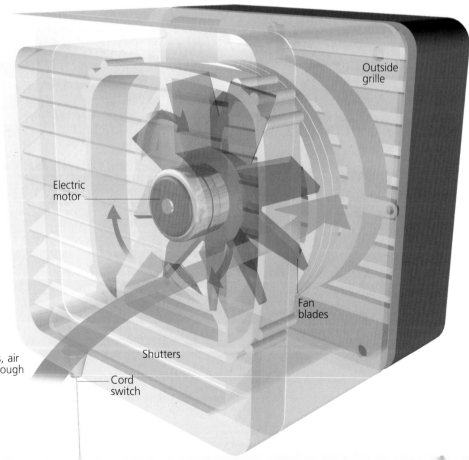

Outside grille

Electric motor

Fan blades

As fan turns, air is drawn through unit to the outside

Shutters

Cord switch

## VENTILATION REGULATIONS

The most important issue when fixing an extractor fan is a source of replaceable air. If a fan is to be fitted in a room with a fuel-burning appliance, building regulations must be adhered to, and wiring must be done in accordance with IEEE (Institute of Electrical & Electronics Engineers) regulations. Ducting must be insulated if it passes through a roof space. If in doubt on any of these issues, always consult a professional electrician.

## Piping air to the outside

Extractor fans can be mounted in walls, windows or ceilings. Fans in bathrooms are often fixed in the ceiling directly above the shower, and the air exits through a duct (wide pipe) in the loft, terminating in an outlet grille. Regulations state that extractor fans must be positioned where they draw the replacement air (usually from the doorway of the room) over the source of the moisture or smells.

There must be no socket outlets in bathrooms, so an extractor must be wired via an FCU, which must not have a switch if it is within reach of the bath or shower – a ceiling switch is used to control the fan if it has no built-in cord pull switch. Where a bathroom does not have an openable window, the extractor must be wired to come on automatically when the light is turned on, and to stay on for at least 15 minutes after it is turned off.

## SAFETY WARNING

Always isolate any appliance from the power supply before carrying out cleaning or maintenance. Remember that DIY repairs to appliances may invalidate your warranty and can be dangerous. Always call an expert if you are in doubt.

## Adjusting the trimmer screw

Extractor fans that are fitted in enclosed bathrooms should run for a minimum of 15 minutes before turning off automatically. To adjust the operating time of the fan, turn off the power to the unit, open the casing and locate the trimmer screw. Adjust the screw according to the manufacturer's instructions.

## FAULT DIAGNOSIS

*Although fans should be connected via an FCU to the mains supply, in some cases this may not have been done in accordance with regulations. If you are in any doubt about isolating the fan, turn off the MCBs (or remove the fuses) for all circuits, then test that the fan has no power before starting any repairs.*

### BROKEN CORD

Replace cord *Some models don't have a cord.*

### FAN RUNNING TIME WRONG

Trimmer out of adjustment *Adjust trimmer screw (above).*

### NOISY OPERATION

Blades catch or shutters rattle *Adjust.*
Motor bearings worn *Have unit replaced.*

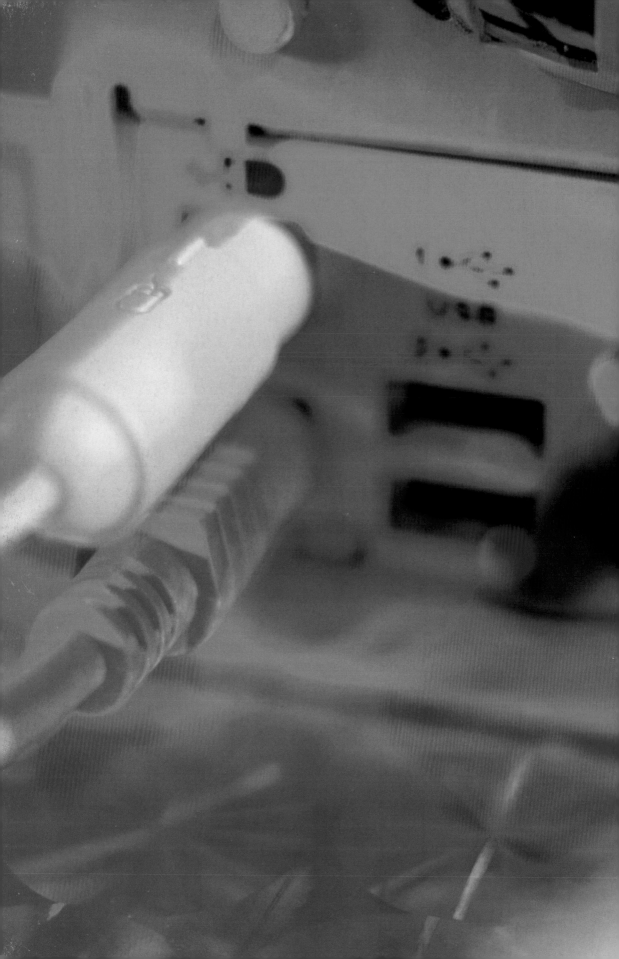

# Audio-visual, computing and communications

# CD player

A compact disc player – whether portable or as part of a home stereo system – uses a laser beam and electronic circuits to read digital data stored on a disc and convert it into sound. CDs are more robust than vinyl records, but can still be affected by dust and scratches, so keep both discs and player clean.

## Caring for your discs

Keeping compact discs clean and free from scratches helps to ensure that the laser beam is reflected accurately off the surface of the CD. It also helps to keep the laser lens within a CD player free from dirt.

## Cleaning CDs

**1** Clean with water and washing-up liquid and a soft lint-free cloth to remove dirt or fingerprints. Rinse and pat dry with a clean lint-free cloth. Wipe from the centre of the disc outwards in straight lines.

**2** Light scratches can sometimes be polished out using a proprietary CD repair kit (above). Buy a reputable brand and follow the instructions explicitly.

### SAFETY WARNING

Never open the CD player case when the power is connected. A CD player uses a laser to read the disc, and laser light can cause damage to eyesight.

## MAINTENANCE

### ONCE A MONTH

**Clean casing of CD player** *Wipe down outside of CD player with dry lint-free cloth. Remove dust and greasy fingerprints. Don't spray furniture polish on unit: use a little on the cloth.*

### EVERY SIX MONTHS

**Clean laser lens with a good-quality lens-cleaning CD** *Follow manufacturer's instructions explicitly. This process may need to be carried out more frequently if there are smokers in the household.*

## FAULT DIAGNOSIS

### NO FUNCTIONS

**No power to appliance** *Check flex, mains supply, plug fuse and wiring for faults. If battery-powered, check batteries. Clean and retension contacts.*

### DISC SPINS INITIALLY BUT WILL NOT PLAY

**Wrong type of CD** *Some CDs, such as those recorded on PCs, will not play in many older CD players. If no discs play, try cleaning the laser lens – see Maintenance.*

### TRACK SKIPPING

**Dirty or scratched disc** *Clean disc.*
**Dirty lens** *See Maintenance.*

### DISC SPINS BUT NO SOUND

**Poor connections** *Check connections between player, amplifier and speakers.*
**Wrong audio source selected** *Check CD player input selected on amplifier.*
**Faulty circuitry** *Contact qualified repairer.*

# Record deck

Fine adjustments to the stylus and its arm have a big impact on the quality of sound produced by a record player. Some simple, regular maintenance will keep the machine – and your vinyl – in good condition.

A rubber drive belt powered by an electric motor turns the platter on which the record is placed. This belt can loosen and start to slip over time, causing the platter to rotate at an uneven speed and the sound produced by the player to be erratic. It may eventually break. Provided you can obtain a replacement part it is a simple job to fit a new one.

The other most common problem with record decks is poor quality of sound, which is often caused by the stylus pressure on the record needing adjustment. The stylus pressure is adjusted by means of a counterweight at the opposite end of the arm. The weight on the record is crucial: too light and the stylus may slip off the record; too heavy and you risk permanently damaging the groove.

## Correcting the stylus pressure

**1** Take off the stylus protector. While supporting the arm, gently turn the counterweight at the opposite end until the arm floats level. Avoid touching the stylus.

**2** Clip the arm back in the C-clip arm rest and, holding the counterweight, turn the stylus pressure ring next to it to zero. Check that the arm still balances.

**3** Check your manual for the correct pressure and turn the counterweight so that the indicated amount appears on the pressure ring.

## MAINTENANCE

### BEFORE EACH USE

Clean stylus *Brush gently towards front of cartridge with stylus brush.*
Clean record *Use cylindrical record brush or antistatic cloth.*

### REGULARLY

Check stylus pressure *If required, adjust counterweight (see below left) to manufacturer's specification.*

## FAULT DIAGNOSIS

### PLATTER DOESN'T TURN

No power *Check mains supply, mains lead, plug and plug fuse.*
Drive belt slipping or broken *Clean or replace belt.*
Controls or switches dirty *Spray with switch cleaner.*
Motor faulty *Contact qualified repairer.*

### POOR SOUND QUALITY

Dirty stylus *Clean stylus. See Maintenance.*
Faulty or worn stylus or cartridge *Replace.*
Stylus pressure incorrect *Adjust stylus pressure (left).*

### CONSTANT HUM

Record player too close to another appliance *Other appliances should be sited at least a metre away.*
Bad connection within cartridge *Check and clean connections.*
Earth wire not connected on amplifier *Connect earth wire's U-shaped connector to screw fitting next to amplifier's phono inputs.*
Faulty cartridge *Replace.*

# Cassette deck

The cassette revolutionised home recording. It made it possible to record and re-record easily onto small cassette tapes, which could be played back at home or on the move. Portable cassette players have been largely replaced by MP3 players, but many home stereo systems and cars still include a cassette deck.

Cassette tape is a long thin strip of plastic coated with an iron-oxide layer which, when exposed to a magnetic field, becomes magnetised. In play or record mode, the pinch roller and capstan drive the tape at a constant speed. The take-up reel is driven by the motor to gather up the slack tape. During playback, the play/record head reads the magnetic signals from the tape and converts them into electric signals. These are then processed into the audio output.

Tapes are not as long-lasting as CDs or records. Over time the tape may stretch or become worn, affecting the sound quality.

## PORTABLE MP3 PLAYERS

Cassette players made music truly portable for the first time, but even their successors, the portable CD player, have now been superseded by digital MP3 players.

With few or no mechanical parts, there are very few repair or maintenance tasks that can be undertaken on these machines by anyone other than a professional. Faults are likely to be software errors that may be corrected using the computer on which the music 'library' is held. To diagnose and fix software problems and hardware faults with your MP3 player it is worth consulting the 'frequently asked questions' page of the manufacturer's website or searching user forums for advice.

## SAFETY WARNING

To prevent the risk of electric shock, always unplug a mains-powered unit before cleaning the pinch rollers.

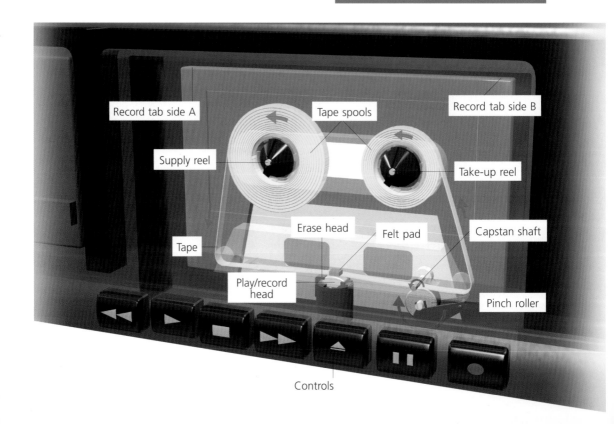

Record tab side A

Tape spools

Record tab side B

Supply reel

Take-up reel

Erase head

Felt pad

Capstan shaft

Tape

Play/record head

Pinch roller

Controls

**SOUND SYSTEMS**

## MAINTENANCE

### ONCE A YEAR

Clean pinch rollers and heads *Keep alcohol away from rubber rollers, and water away from electrical circuits.*
Demagnetise heads *Use a proprietary head cleaner to clean heads.*

## FAULT DIAGNOSIS

### NOTHING FUNCTIONS

Fuse or wiring fault *Check plug fuse and plug wiring for faults.*
Flat battery *If battery-powered, check and replace batteries. Clean battery contacts and pull contacts slightly forward so they have a firm grip on the batteries.*

### POOR PLAYBACK

Dirty tape path *Clean pinch roller, capstan shaft and heads.*
Heads magnetised *Use a head cleaner to demagnetise heads.*
Head misaligned *Contact qualified repairer.*

### NOISY WINDING

Tape faulty *Try another cassette.*
Reel shafts need lubricating *Put a drop of light machine oil onto each shaft.*

### UNEVEN PLAYBACK

Tape loose or twisted in cassette *Pull a little slack tape from cassette and then wind reels manually with pen or pencil. Do not put very twisted tape into machine: it could jam.*
Stretched tape *C120s are very thin and tend to stretch so are unsuitable for repeated use.*

## Cleaning pinch rollers and heads

**1** Use isopropyl alcohol to clean the capstan shaft and a cotton bud dipped in soapy water to clean the pinch rollers.

**2** To clean the heads, dip a clean cotton bud in isopropyl alcohol, squeeze out any excess drops and then rub it gently across the surface.

## Oiling the shaft

Lay the cassette deck on its side and run a single drop of light machine oil down a needle directly onto the shaft of each reel.

## Demagnetising heads

Commercially available tape head demagnetisers help to maximise playback and record quality. Always follow the manufacturer's instructions.

# Amplifier

The electrical signals produced by CD players, record or tape decks are too weak to drive loudspeakers directly. They need to be boosted by an amplifier, which may be an integral part of the machine or separate.

Electrical signals from the CD player, tuner or other audio source enter the amplifier via the input sockets on the rear panel. Volume, balance and tone control is applied to both stereo channels before the signal is amplified until it is powerful enough to drive a set of loudspeakers. This is then delivered as an output signal. If a stand-alone amplifier does not seem to be working always check first that the correct audio source is selected.

## MAKE THE RATINGS MATCH

Amplifiers have two important ratings: the output power is measured in watts RMS (root mean square). A rating of 20W+20W RMS means that each channel can continuously deliver 20 watts of power to each speaker. The impedance rating refers to the resistance of the speakers that are connected to it. Make sure that your speakers have the same power and impedance ratings as your amplifier, or damage may occur.

## Cleaning switches

Turn the amplifier off and disconnect it from the mains supply. Remove the top cover and locate the position of switches and volume control. Spray switch cleaner into the component and twiddle the control knob to help to clean the contact.

## FAULT DIAGNOSIS

*If there is a fault with the sound output from your speakers, check that the symptom is the same when you use headphones. If it is, the amplifier is faulty. If it is not, one or both of the speakers must be faulty.*

### NO FUNCTIONS

No power *Check flex, plug fuse and wiring for faults.*
Internal fuse blown *Fuse must be replaced. Contact qualified repairer.*

### NO SOUND FROM SPEAKERS (LEDs LIT)

Wrong audio source *Switch to correct source.*
Speakers not turned on *Check speaker switches.*
Speakers not connected *Check speakers are wired correctly to amplifier.*
Internal fuse blown *Contact qualified repairer.*
Headphones plugged in *Unplug.*

### NO OUTPUT ON ONE CHANNEL

Balance control offset *Adjust.*
Faulty speaker connection *Swap connections.*
Speaker or amplifier faulty *Swap speakers – if fault persists, contact qualified repairer or replace speaker.*

### CRACKLING WHEN ADJUSTING VOLUME

Dirty controls *Clean with switch cleaner (see left).*

### DISTORTED SOUND

Faulty speaker(s) *Confirm fault by checking with headphones.*
Faulty audio source *Switch to another input source. If problem persists, audio source is not at fault.*
Faulty internal circuitry *Contact qualified repairer.*

# Loudspeaker

The electrical signals generated by an amplifier are turned into sound waves via a loudspeaker. A simple magnet and moving coil are used to transform electrical pulses into the vibration of a thin cone, which moves backwards and forwards to create sound waves.

Most small loudspeakers have two speakers inside the box – a standard speaker, for low and mid-range frequencies, and a 'tweeter' for high frequencies. A device called a passive crossover unit splits the high and low frequencies and routes them to the appropriate speaker.

The speaker cabinet is designed to minimise unwanted vibration and resonances. In a bass reflex speaker there is a tuned porthole to increase the bass response. A speaker's sound, particularly the base, is only as good as the cable that carries the signal, so always buy the best you can afford that is suitable for your equipment and try to avoid making joins.

Speakers have a rating called impedance, which is measured in ohms (typically 4–15 ohms). They also have a power rating in watts. Both ratings should match the amplifier that feeds them. If speakers are under-rated, damage may occur to speakers and amplifier if used at high volume. If speakers are over-rated, then the amplifier may not be able to drive them efficiently.

## Checking connections

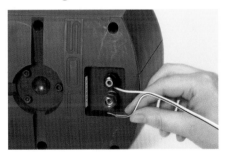

Speaker wires may be red and black or one cable may have a stripe (as above). Connect the red or striped wire to the red (positive) connector on the amplifier and the black to the black (negative). Connect the red or striped cable to the red connector on the speaker, and the black cable to the black connector.

---

### MAINTENANCE

#### EVERY SIX MONTHS

Clean speaker cones and inside of cabinet *Dust can build up, especially on large cones, and eventually cause problems with sound quality.*

---

### FAULT DIAGNOSIS

#### NO SOUND ON ONE CHANNEL

Balance not centred *Check amplifier balance setting.*
Speakers not connected correctly *Check speaker connections and cables. Remake connections as necessary.*
One speaker damaged *Swap speakers over to confirm that speaker is faulty. Replace speaker.*

#### DISTORTION OR LOW SOUND

Wrong rating for amplifier *Confirm speakers are correctly rated for amplifier – replace speakers if not.*
Speaker fault *Swap speakers. If same speaker still shows symptom, replace speakers with correct rating. Otherwise amplifier may be faulty – consult qualified repairer.*

#### POOR BASS RESPONSE

Poor-quality cable *Replace.*
Speakers not connected correctly *Check speaker connection – reverse one connection if necessary.*

---

### SAFETY WARNING

Always unplug, disconnect or isolate any equipment when carrying out cleaning, repairs or maintenance.

# Television set

Whether you have a bulky CRT (cathode ray tube) set or a more modern flat-panel model using either plasma or LCD technology, TV repairs should always be left to a professional, but it is worth knowing how to keep your set in good condition.

Programmes reach your TV via an analogue or digital signal received using an aerial, cable or satellite system (see page 114). Regardless of how the signal is received, the image is decoded and split into its red, green and blue components for display on the screen, and the sound is separated and routed to an amplifier and speakers.

Cathode ray tube (CRT) televisions have been around since the birth of television. Beams of electrons are fired from heated filaments, or cathodes, within a glass container known as the cathode ray tube and are focused to form a picture on the screen. It is this tube that makes these models so deep and bulky. Modern flat-panel alternatives have very little depth, but can be produced with very large screen sizes, up to 80in for plasma and 50in for LCD models. (Screen sizes are measured in inches, diagonally from corner to corner.)

## MOVING A TELEVISION

Always carry a television set with the screen facing towards you – in a CRT set this is the heaviest part and this technique will put the least strain on your back and help to prevent you from losing your balance. Always hold the plug and cable well away from the floor to prevent tripping as you walk.

Despite being less bulky in depth, plasma screens of any size and large-screen-size LCDs are very heavy pieces of equipment and will require two people to lift them safely.

## Flat-panel options

With the benefits of reduced bulk, there are also some disadvantages. Plasma televisions are very heavy and if you plan to mount one on a wall or from a ceiling you must follow the manufacturer's instructions. They are easily damaged by careless handling and can suffer from a condition known as 'burn in' if a stationary image is left on screen for a long period. The after image, or 'ghost' effect, is permanent, so never leave a programme paused on-screen for a long time. Plasma screens have a life span of between 30,000 and 40,000 hours (around 3½ years of continuous use). They use significantly more power and produce more heat than their LCD equivalents.

LCD models do not suffer from 'burn in' but can have 'stuck pixels', which results in small dots of one colour being permanently displayed. LCD screens weigh much less than their plasma equivalents and are more robust, but care must still be taken when moving them. The life span of LCD televisions is similar to plasma sets. The back light, which is used to produce the images on screen, can be renewed to extend the set's life, but this is a job for a professional television engineer and may not be cost effective.

## Cables and connections

The latest televisions are capable of producing very high quality images, but the images can only be as good as the cables used to carry the signals. Always choose the best leads you can afford, particularly if you have a plasma or LCD set. Avoid using long leads to transmit analogue signals, as the signal will degrade over distance (this is not a problem with a digital signal). Try to avoid routing power and signal leads close together, as this can result in problems for both analogue and digital signals. Check all the connections to the back of the television regularly and try to ensure that there is always a little slack in the lead to avoid connections being put under strain. Make sure that no connections are being pushed against the wall or another piece of equipment.

## SAFETY WARNING

Some internal components of televisions carry potentially lethal voltages, even when unplugged. Never remove the casing from your television. Leave all internal repair work to a qualified TV engineer.

## FAULT DIAGNOSIS

### NO FUNCTIONS

No power *Check plug wiring, fuse and mains socket outlet for faults.*

### NO PICTURE

Transmitter failure *Check on another TV set.*
Aerial or other input cable loose *Check all connectors.*
Wrong input selected *Make sure TV is set to correct input.*
Un-programmed channel selected or TV not tuned in *Select correct channel number or retune TV.*
If sound OK: internal fault *Turn off set and contact qualified repairer.*

### WEAK SIGNAL ('SNOW' ON SCREEN)

Poorly tuned channel *Check other channels. Retune if necessary.*
Poor aerial signal *Check cables, connections and aerial alignment. Consult qualified aerial installer.*

### NO SOUND

Volume down or on mute *Check.*
Station not tuned in *Retune.*

### COLOURED PATCH ON SCREEN (CRT)

Shadow mask is magnetised *A magnetic source, eg loudspeaker, is too close to set. Move speakers away from TV and demagnetise (degauss) the screen. Turn set on for 30 seconds then off for half an hour. Repeat three times.*

## MAINTENANCE

*Always use a television as indicated in the manufacturer's manual. Never attempt to connect it in any way other than instructed.*

### EVERY WEEK

Clean the screen and rear of the unit *High static charge on screen attracts dust.*
Clean the remote control with a slightly damp cloth *See remote control, page 111.*

## Cleaning the set

The screen surface of any television can be easily damaged and it is a good idea to use a specialist cleaning kit, as you would for an expensive camera lens. CRT and plasma screens, although made of glass, are coated with an anti-glare coating that can be damaged by inappropriate cleaning solutions or materials. An LCD screen (and a flat-panel computer monitor screen, above) is a soft film that is easily scratched by misuse and incorrect cleaning. Use a large looped microfibre cleaning cloth with the minimum of pressure to clean the screen. Do not use anything but high-quality liquid cleaners designed specifically for screen-cleaning and use only when needed. Apply the cleaning liquid liberally onto the cloth, but never directly to the screen. Do not use tissues, paper kitchen towel, hand towels or cloths for general cleaning, as these may have abrasives that can scratch the screen's surface.

# Video recorder

The VHS video cassette recorder (VCR) is one of the most complex devices in the home. It combines precisely aligned mechanical parts with sophisticated electronic circuits to record pictures and sound onto tape. However, despite its complexity, the VCR is a reliable and long-lived machine, and is easily kept in peak condition.

## SAFETY WARNING

Always unplug, disconnect or isolate any appliance when carrying out cleaning, repairs or maintenance.

## THE TAPE PATH

When the cassette is lowered into the machine, two rollers ❶ are positioned behind the tape. A tensioning arm ❷ is also in place, ready to rotate and press the tape against the erase head ❸ . When the tape loads, the rollers both move towards the rotating record/play head ❹ , wrapping the tape around the head. The pinch roller ❺ moves toward the capstan ❻ and the tensioning arm swings out, creating the correct tape tension.

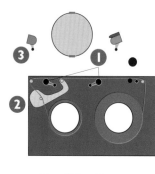

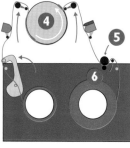

A video cassette is similar to an audio cassette, in that the information is recorded onto magnetic tape. During recording, an eraser head removes any previously recorded material from the tape. Two rotating video heads each record one half of the television signal. The tape then passes an audio record head, which lays down a sound track.

In playback, the magnetically recorded video information is read by the rotating heads and the audio track is read by the audio heads. The video and audio signals are combined and sent to a TV by S-video or SCART connection (see page 110).

## MAINTENANCE

### EVERY THREE MONTHS

**Clean heads** *Use a good quality head-cleaning video cassette to clean heads and rollers. Always follow the manufacturer's instructions and replace pads and liquid at the recommended intervals.*
**Clean casing** *Keep the outside of VCR free from dust by wiping down with lint-free cloth. Don't spray furniture polish directly onto unit.*

### ONCE A YEAR

**Clean tape path** *Open case and clean route where tape runs during operation (see opposite).*

## RECORDING FORMATS

American videos are recorded in a different format from UK videos and will only play on UK machines if the unit is 'NTSC compatible'. Consult your manual to find out which formats your VCR can play.

## Cleaning inside the recorder

**1** Turn off and unplug the VCR. Remove the case screws and lift off the cover. Clean the pinch roller with a slightly soaped cotton bud. Clean the capstan and any static heads (but not the video head drum) using a cotton swab dipped in pure isopropyl alcohol.

**2** Use a chamois-tipped swab (available from electronics outlets) to clean the erase head. Aerosol head-cleaning fluid can be used to remove stubborn deposits.

## Removing a jammed cassette

Unplug the VCR and remove the cover. Carefully try to turn the tape mechanism cog (if present) manually to eject the tape. If the tape is tangled in the mechanism, carefully cut it free first. Also, check the cassette carriage for obstructions in the mechanism. If in any doubt, consult a qualified repairer.

## FAULT DIAGNOSIS

*Do not use a video cassette if the picture is poor. If dirty heads are to blame, then the tape may be damaged, and if the tape is worn it may deposit oxide onto the heads. Over time, permanent damage can be caused to the VCR by dirty tapes and heads.*

### VCR DOESN'T WORK

No power *Check switches, cables and plug fuse for faults.*
Moisture in mechanism *Look for 'dew warning' light. Move VCR away from condensation source and allow to acclimatise for up to three hours.*

### CASSETTE JAMMED

Warped cassette *Unplug VCR, open case and carefully try to free the cassette by working it loose.*
Object blocking eject system *Open case and carefully remove blockage.*

### POOR PICTURE QUALITY

Low quality tape *Try another tape. If it works, throw first one away and clean heads.*
Dirty heads *Clean heads and rollers with a good-quality head-cleaning video cassette. Always follow manufacturer's instructions.*
Tracking out of alignment *Check VCR operating manual for instructions on how to adjust tracking or reset automatic tracking.*
Poor connections *Check connectors and cables between the VCR and TV.*
TV not tuned correctly *Refer to manual.*

### TAPES DAMAGED BY MACHINE

Poor quality tape *Discard tape.*
Tape guides need adjusting *Contact qualified repairer.*
Dirty tape path *Clean inside unit.*
Faulty mechanism *Contact qualified repairer.*

# Audio-visual connecting leads

Connecting audio components together or wiring a video, DVD player or games console to a TV can involve using several different types of lead. Choosing the right connector for the job is vital for your appliances to work properly.

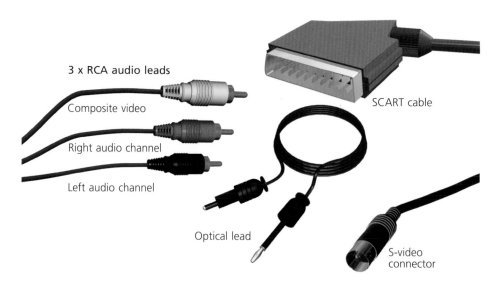

3 x RCA audio leads

Composite video

Right audio channel

Left audio channel

SCART cable

Optical lead

S-video connector

## Know your connectors

### RCA audio leads
RCA (Radio Company of America) leads are normally used to connect audio equipment such as a CD or cassette player to an amplifier. They comprise simple leads, known as coaxial leads because they have a central conductive core wrapped in an outer conducting layer. They are normally in pairs – for left and right signal connections to an amplifier – or with an extra yellow RCA cable for a composite video signal.

### SCART cables
SCART (Syndicat des Constructeurs d'Appareils Radiorécepteurs et Téléviseurs) is a versatile lead and connector, used to link video devices to one another or to a television. Always use a fully-wired SCART lead, which can transmit a signal that switches the TV from standby mode and changes the screen from 4:3 to 16:9 for widescreen broadcasts.

### Optical leads
These carry digital information and are normally used between CD players and MiniDisc recorders. A laser light carries audio information along a fibre-optic lead with no loss of quality, as there is no need to convert the signal from digital to analogue and back.

## Types of video signal

### Composite
The red, green and blue components of a video signal are combined and transmitted down a single RCA lead. This signal does not include sound. Composite signals can also be transmitted though a SCART cable.

### S-video (super video)
This produces a clearer picture on a television than a composite signal. The video signal is split into two channels: colour and brightness. S-video signals can be transmitted down a special S-video cable, or through a SCART lead.

### RGB (red, green, blue)
This is the best way of transmitting a video signal between devices. The red, green and blue parts of a colour TV signal are carried by individual leads within a fully wired SCART cable, which also carries the sound.

### KEEP LEADS TIDY

Make sure all leads are away from areas where people walk, and are neatly arranged. Use lead ties and routing channels if necessary.

# Remote control

A remote control uses pulses of infrared light to control audio-visual systems: changing a TV channel, adjusting the volume, or selecting tracks on a CD player. Dirt and grease from fingers can build up over time, so keeping it clean will help to keep it working.

Keypad

Infrared transmitter

Printed circuit board

Batteries

As a button is pressed on the remote control, a conductive contact completes a circuit with a printed circuit board. The connection is detected by a processor on the circuit board, which generates a code representing the button that was pressed.

The processor sends the code to an infrared transmitter. This is an LED (light emitting diode) that sends out a beam of infrared light, which is picked up by a sensor in the device to be controlled. An electronic circuit decodes the sequence and performs the function.

## Cleaning the buttons

Remove the battery compartment cover and remove any screws with a small screwdriver. Open the casing and carefully lift off the rubber keypad and clean the top surface with a damp soapy cloth. Clean the undersides of the keys with a dry, lint-free cloth and a little isopropyl alcohol. Replace keypad, screws and battery cover.

### FAULT DIAGNOSIS

#### NO FUNCTIONS AT ALL

No battery power *Test batteries in another device. Clean and re-tension remote battery contacts.*
Remote not working *Tune a radio to medium wave and find a quiet gap between stations. Hold the remote near the radio and press a button. If the remote is working, a high-pitched sound will be heard.*

#### LED FLASHES BUT RECEIVING UNIT DOESN'T RESPOND

Receiving unit faulty or not turned on *If applicable, follow manufacturer's instructions for resetting unit.*

#### SOME BUTTONS STICKING OR NOT FUNCTIONING

Dirt inside unit *Clean keypad. Be careful when opening case, as the keys are all separate in some remote controls. Make sure no moisture is left on the remote control, and do not use abrasive cleaning products.*

TELEVISION AND VIDEO

# DVD player

A single-sided, single-layer digital versatile disc (DVD) can store more than six times the data capacity of a standard CD-ROM. This is enough space for more than two hours of sound and video, including subtitles and additional information.

A DVD player works in a similar way to a compact disc player (see CD player, page 100). A drive motor spins the disc as a tracking mechanism moves a laser and lens assembly over the disc's surface. Digital data – sound, video, subtitles and menu information – stored on the disc is read, decoded and sent to the television, where it is displayed on screen and played through the loudspeakers.

Some DVDs have a second layer. This starts at the outside of the disc, allowing the laser to quickly focus on a different layer without the lens assembly having to move back to the centre of the disc. The DVD player adjusts for single or double-layer playing automatically.

All DVDs contain a recorded code, which is read by the decoder and specifies the region in which the disc will play. There are six regions covering the entire globe. Modern DVD players can play discs from more than one region, but with older models a DVD from one region will not play in a player from another.

## Playing and recording

Many DVD players are now also able to record programmes and they are quickly taking over from the VCR as the most popular choice for home video recording. DVD-R discs can only be used once, but DVD-RW can be recorded and rewritten many times without loss of quality.

New technology is constantly increasing the maximum record time and introducing new features, but the basic repair and maintenance tasks remain the same.

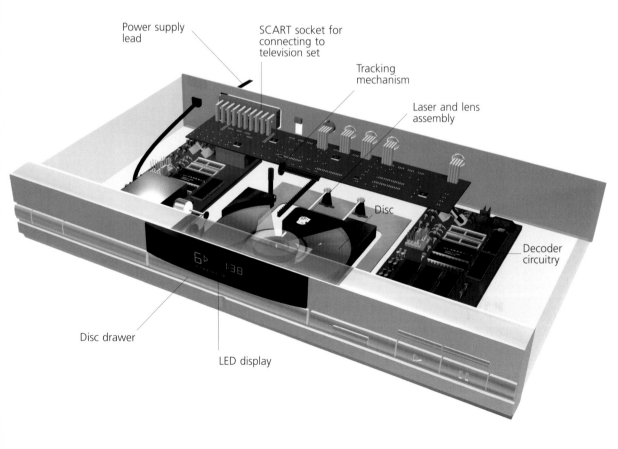

Power supply lead

SCART socket for connecting to television set

Tracking mechanism

Laser and lens assembly

Disc

Decoder circuitry

Disc drawer

LED display

## DVD TRACKS

The laser mechanism in a DVD player has to be much more accurate than in a CD player. This is because the tracks on a DVD are closer together, the bumps are smaller, and the data may be on two layers, requiring the laser mechanism ❶ to focus through the first layer ❷ to read the second ❸. To read the layers on a double-sided disc, the disc must be turned over.

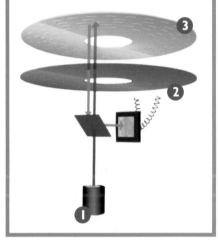

## Cleaning the lens

Obtain a reputable make of lens-cleaning disc. Follow the manufacturer's instructions carefully. Place the disc in the drive as instructed and press play. The tiny brushes remove dust and debris from the lens area.

## MAINTENANCE

### WHEN REQUIRED

Keep DVD discs clean *See Compact disc player, page 100.*

### TWICE YEARLY

Clean laser lens *Use a good quality propriety lens cleaning CD.*

## SAFETY WARNING

**Always unplug or disconnect any appliance when carrying out cleaning or maintenance. DIY repairs can be dangerous and may invalidate your warranty. Consult a qualified repairer if you are in doubt.**

## FAULT DIAGNOSIS

### NO FUNCTIONS

Power supply problem *Check plug wiring, fuse and mains supply.*

### NO PICTURE OR NO SOUND

Poor connection to TV *Check SCART connections on television and DVD player are secure. If this does not work, consult qualified repairer.*

### NO DISCS PLAY

Dirty laser lens *Clean laser lens. Use a good quality propriety lens cleaning CD.If this fails, consult qualified repairer.*

### CAN'T PLAY A DISC

DVD has wrong region code for your player *Check code on DVD box and compare with instruction manual for DVD player.*

# Digital TV decoder

**Several delivery methods have been developed to cope with the huge data capacity that is required to transmit digital pictures and sound. One of the most successful of these media is satellite television, whereby digital signals are received by a small dish mounted on the roof or house wall in place of a conventional aerial, and decoded via a set-top box linked to the television set.**

A dish picks up all available signals from the satellite and feeds them to a tuner and decoder in the set-top box. In a simple receiver, the user can select a single channel to be viewed. Other receivers allow one signal to be watched while another is recorded and some contain a hard drive to record and store programmes either manually or automatically.

The video and audio signals are decoded and fed to the television via a SCART socket (see Audio-visual connecting leads, page 110). Under normal conditions, the picture and sound quality is higher than that produced by analogue TV systems.

The digital broadcast also carries more information. An on-screen menu allows the viewer to change preferences, quickly scan through programme guides and select channels.

A SMART card, working in conjunction with software in the receiver, determines the recipient's entitlement to view any given channel and the ability of the receiver to unscramble the signal. Several channels are freely available, but certain channels (such as films and sport) require the purchase of additional subscription packages. These are controlled by the service provider via the SMART card.

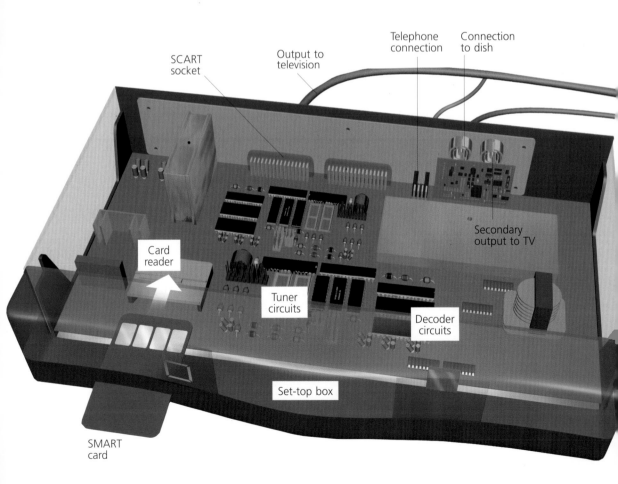

SCART socket

Output to television

Telephone connection

Connection to dish

Secondary output to TV

Card reader

Tuner circuits

Decoder circuits

Set-top box

SMART card

## Connecting the set-top box

The satellite receiver box needs to be permanently connected to a telephone line so that it can communicate with the service provider. If you have broadband internet access, you must fit an ADSL filter to the set-top box's telephone connection, just as you would with any other telephone in the house. (See Wiring for home computers, page 123.)

When the viewer uses an interactive service (such as a game), a modem in the receiver dials the provider's computer, in a similar way to connecting to the internet. During this time, the user's telephone line will be engaged to incoming callers. However, if the user picks up the telephone to make a call, the box will release the line.

If the viewer selects a 'pay per view' film or programme, this information is stored in the decoder and sent to the provider via the telephone connection at an off-peak time. The charge appears on the next telephone bill, unless it is a premium service, in which case information about the additional cost of these calls will be displayed prior to connection.

Parental restrictions can be applied to the unit to stop children going online without an adult's permission. This involves setting up a PIN code, which must be entered before the box will allow access to interactive services.

### LOOKING AFTER CABLES

Make sure all cables are tucked safely out of the way. Use cable ties to keep them tidy. Check that the SCART cable is plugged firmly into the receiver and the back of the VCR or TV. If necessary, remove the cable from both sockets and reinsert it carefully.

### FAULT DIAGNOSIS

#### NO FUNCTIONS

No power *Check plug fuse, flex and socket outlet for faults.*
Poor signal to decoder *A weak digital signal cannot be decoded, so no picture will display. If signal is from an aerial, try adding a booster. If signal is from a satellite dish, consult a qualified satellilte installer.*

#### ON-SCREEN ERROR MESSAGE

No signal received *Check cable connections and check for damaged or kinked cable.*
Dish misaligned or receiver faulty *Consult supplier.*
Decoder 'locked' or crashed *This is often the result of a power failure. Turn off the decoder, wait for 30 seconds then turn back on again.*
Incorrect viewing card or slot being used *Check that your viewing card is valid and inserted the right way round in the correct slot.*

#### BLOCKY OR POOR QUALITY SIGNAL

Dish misaligned *Consult supplier.*
Cable/receiver faulty *Consult supplier.*
Interrupted line of sight between dish and satellite *Adverse weather conditions may cause this temporarily. It may also indicate that the dish is slightly off alignment. Contact supplier if symptoms persist.*
Receiver overheating *Ensure adequate ventilation.*
Processor in receiver locked up (picture freezes or can't access different channels) *Switch off mains power to set-top receiver for a few seconds. If this does not work, reset receiver (consult supplier for precise sequence).*

#### VIDEO OR SOUND INTERMITTENT

Faulty connections *Check connections between receiver and VCR/TV.*

# Keyboard

**The keyboard is a computer's primary input device. Regular cleaning will prolong its useful life.**

A computer keyboard is not just for typing characters; certain key combinations and special keys enable the user to control the functions of a computer and its programs. In fact, a computer is of no use to anyone without its keyboard. So it is worth keeping the keyboard in good working order.

## Cleaning the keyboard

Turn off the computer. Spray the cleaning product onto a cloth, and wipe the keys and case gently to remove dirt. Use a lint-free or foam cotton bud to carefully clean in between the keys.

| MAINTENANCE |
|---|
| **AS REQUIRED, DEPENDING ON USE** |
| Remove debris from within keyboard *Turn keyboard upside down over bin, and tap to dislodge debris from under keys. For spilt drinks, turn upside down over bucket and leave to dry.*<br>Clean keyboard *Use proprietary computer keyboard cleaning product to remove grease and dirt from keys.* |

| FAULT DIAGNOSIS |
|---|
| **KEYBOARD NOT WORKING** |
| Cables dislodged *Check connections and restart computer.* |
| **KEY STUCK** |
| Key jammed *Carefully lever key from keyboard. Make sure it doesn't fly out. Replace by clipping in position.* |

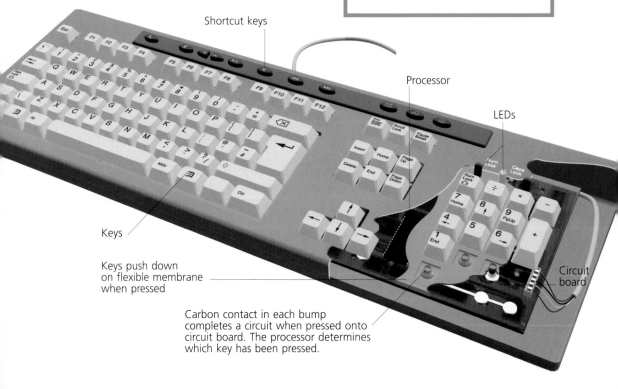

Shortcut keys

Processor

LEDs

Keys

Keys push down on flexible membrane when pressed

Circuit board

Carbon contact in each bump completes a circuit when pressed onto circuit board. The processor determines which key has been pressed.

# Mouse

A mouse is used to control the movement of a computer's on-screen pointer. Depending on where the pointer is positioned, clicking the mouse gives the computer a variety of instructions.

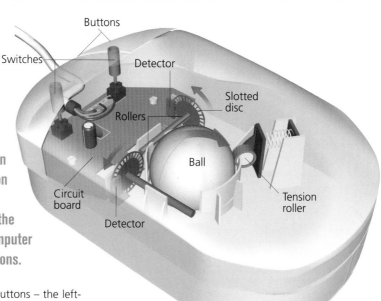

Buttons
Switches
Detector
Slotted disc
Rollers
Ball
Circuit board
Detector
Tension roller

A PC mouse has two buttons – the left-hand one selects on-screen items and the right-hand button displays drop down menus. An AppleMac mouse usually has just one button. Some mice also have a scroll wheel to allow the user to rapidly move up and down a page. As the mouse is moved around the mat, a ball in its base turns two rollers connected to slotted discs that rotate past detectors. These measure the motion of the ball, which is converted into the horizontal and vertical motion of the cursor on the monitor.

There are other types of mice. An optical mouse detects movement using a bright light-emitting diode (LED) and sensors. As the mouse is moved, changes in the way light from the LED is reflected beneath it are detected and interpreted. A cordless mouse uses a ball, but transmits radio signals in place of electrical ones.

## FAULT DIAGNOSIS

### MOUSE NOT WORKING

Cables dislodged *Check connections and reboot computer.*

### CURSOR JUMPING

Dirty rollers *Clean ball and rollers.*
Settings incorrect *Change settings on your computer.*

### MOUSE ERRATIC

Cordless mouse batteries flat *Replace batteries.*
Cordless mouse receiver displaced *Move receiver.*

## MAINTENANCE

### ONCE A MONTH

Clean mouse ball and rollers *Dirt and dust can build up on rollers, causing erratic pointer motion.*

## Cleaning the mouse

**1** Turn off the computer and remove the panel on the base of the mouse. Lift out the ball and clean the rollers with a cotton bud dipped in isopropyl alcohol. Use a soft plastic tool on stubborn deposits.

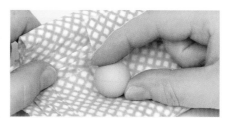

**2** Wipe the ball with a soft damp cloth. Wait for the ball to dry then reassemble the mouse and turn the computer back on.

# Printers

**Ink-jet printers are the most popular choice for home computers. Essentially they work by spraying droplets of ink onto paper from hundreds of tiny nozzles. The ink is supplied in cartridges, which are easy to replace when they run out.**

Ink-jet printers are easier to run and maintain than laser printers, which tend to be better for the heavier usage required in offices. When checking for problems in your ink-jet printer, it helps to have an understanding of how it works.

When a document is sent to print, the paper feed moves a sheet of paper from the paper tray to position it under the print head. The paper feed stepper motor is synchronised with the print head stepper motor so that the print head is positioned accurately over the paper.

Microscopic ink droplets are drawn from the ink cartridge and then precisely targeted onto the paper by the print head.

In some printers, the print head is integrated into the ink cartridge. A stabiliser bar ensures the print head remains the correct distance above the paper. This bar can be raised by a lever to prevent smudging if thicker paper is used.

As the print head is moved across the page, it stops every fraction of a second to spray dots of ink onto the paper. The speed and quality of the printing is determined by the dpi (dots per inch) setting. The higher the dpi, the slower the print job and the better the quality.

When the width of the page has been covered, the paper feed stepper motor moves the paper along a small amount. The print head then reverses direction, pausing and printing as it goes. The process of stopping and starting is so quick that the print head appears to move continuously.

When the whole page has been printed, the print head is returned to the park position and the paper feed stepper motor rolls the paper out of the printer.

Paper tray

Print head and pressurised ink cartridges

Print head stepper motor

Stabiliser bar lever

Drive belt

Park position

Paper

Stabiliser bar

Paper feed stepper motor

## MAINTENANCE

### ONCE A MONTH

Perform self-test and self-cleaning *Check manual for instructions.*

### BEFORE FITTING NEW INK CARTRIDGE

Remove paper debris from feed path *Fit new cartridge as described in manual.*

## Checking the print head

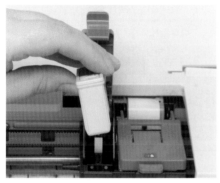

Move the cartridge to its park or installation position and unclip it. Lift out the cartridge and check for protective covers or tapes. Check the manufacturer's manual for instructions if you are unsure how to do this. Remove any protective tapes or plastic covers and refit the cartridge.

## SAFETY WARNING

Always switch off and unplug any electrical appliance when carrying out cleaning or maintenance. DIY repairs may invalidate your warranty and can be dangerous. Always call an expert if in doubt. In some cases, replacing the printer will be more cost effective than making a repair.

## FAULT DIAGNOSIS

### SMUDGED INK

Poor-quality paper *Always use correct paper for printer.*
Paper too thick *Raise print head using stabiliser bar lever. Return to normal position when using standard paper.*
Dirty heads *Perform self-clean. If symptom persists, contact qualified repairer.*

### UNUSED CARTRIDGE BUT NO INK

Dirty heads *Perform self-clean. If symptom persists, contact qualified repairer.*
Heads dried out *Replace cartridge.*
Protective tape left on print head *Remove tape and protective covers.*

### ODD CHARACTERS ON PAGE

Wrong printer selected *If more than one printer installed in Windows® printers folder, check correct one has been selected. If there is only one printer, make it the default printer. Delete unused printers from folder.*
Corrupted driver *Reinstall printer driver from manufacturer's CD-ROM or website.*
Upgraded operating system *If new operating system does not have correct driver, obtain one from printer manufacturer. Many can be downloaded from the internet.*

### POOR PRINT QUALITY

Dirty heads *Perform self-clean. If symptom persists, contact qualified repairer.*

### WARNING LIGHTS FLASHING

Fault detected by printer *Check documentation supplied with printer.*

# Computer connecting leads

It is possible to connect a wide range of peripheral devices to a computer – from printers and scanners to mobile phones and even sewing machines. However, as digital technology has developed, the ports and connection types have changed as well, requiring new styles of lead, plug and socket.

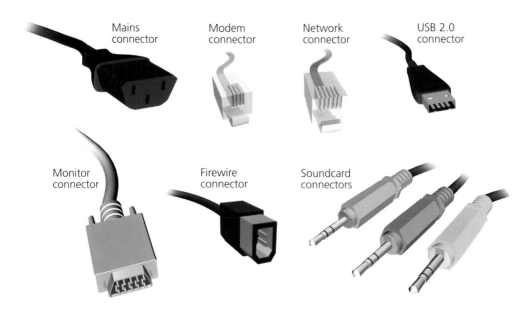

Mains connector

Modem connector

Network connector

USB 2.0 connector

Monitor connector

Firewire connector

Soundcard connectors

### Mains connector
To avoid damaging the computer, the mains voltage selector needs to be set to 110V or 230V. Choose 230V for use in the UK.

### PS/2 ports
PS/2 ports are used on older PCs to connect the keyboard and mouse. They are colour-coded or marked with icons.

### Serial ports
Serial (COM) ports are used on older PCs for modems and mice. However, they have now been superseded by USB connections.

### Parallel ports
Parallel ports are faster than serial ports, but they, too, have beeen largely replaced by USB connections. Some scanners and printers still use parallel connections.

### USB connector
Most modern computers have at least two USB 2.0 ports available at the rear; some models have up to six on the back and two on the front. These are very fast serial ports, but, unlike serial (COM) ports, they allow devices to be plugged in or removed while the computer is running. Some devices, such as printers, feature smaller or differently shaped USB ports, but these will come supplied with the correct cables and it is easy to see which end fits where.

### FireWire connector
These high-speed serial connections are now used on many new PCs. Nearly all digital camcorders and some MP3 players use FireWire to connect. There are several types of connector available so make sure you get the right cable for your PC and device. If your PC does not have a FireWire port, you can install a FireWire card or an external FireWire and USB 2.0 hub.

### Modem connector
The modem is what your computer uses to connect to a telephone line in order to access the internet.

### SETTING UP YOUR PC

Make sure all cables are tucked safely out of the way, using cable ties to keep them tidy. It is a good idea to fit a surge protector to your PC's power socket to protect the computer against a power surge.

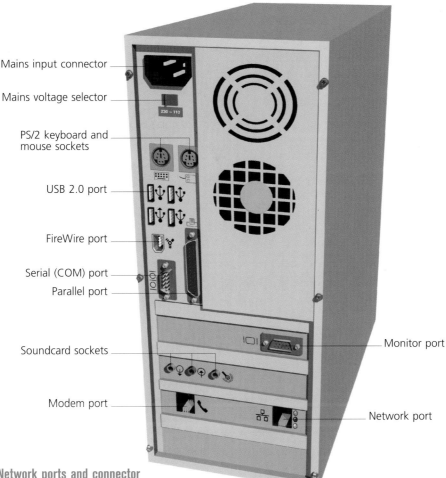

Mains input connector

Mains voltage selector

PS/2 keyboard and mouse sockets

USB 2.0 port

FireWire port

Serial (COM) port

Parallel port

Soundcard sockets

Modem port

Monitor port

Network port

### Network ports and connector

All modern computers have network cards. These allow you to connect to another computer or network to share information and hardware. Network ports also enable PCs to be connected to a broadband modem or router. The correct cable should be supplied with the hardware – press the tag on the plug when unplugging and take care not to confuse the modem and network connections, as they are similar.

### Monitor connector

The monitor plugs into a dedicated port, which is attached to a graphics card or directly to the motherboard.

### Soundcard connections

The soundcard will usually have sockets for speakers (line out), line in and microphone. These may be colour coded or marked with icons to make wiring them easy. Here, the speaker connections are green, line-in is blue and the microphone is pink.

### Wireless network cards

These use radio waves to connect to wireless networks, broadband modems or routers. Most are invisible when built into a laptop, but a wireless network card for a desktop PC may have a short aerial.

## FAULT DIAGNOSIS

### NO FUNCTIONS

No power *Check power supply and connections.*
Data cable disconnected *Check and refit.*
Cable damaged *Check and replace.*

### NO SCREEN DISPLAY – LEDS ON COMPUTER LIT NORMALLY

No power to monitor *Check power supply and connections to computer.*

### NETWORK CONNECTION FAILS

Network cable unplugged *Refit cables.*
Computer problem *Restart all computers on network. If this fails, contact qualified repairer.*

# Telephone wiring

**Although most of the faults connected with your domestic telephone line will have to be dealt with by a telephone engineer, there are a few measures you can undertake yourself to keep your telephone system on line.**

The internal workings of a telephone are complicated and best not tampered with, but it is fairly straightforward to add extension cables and sockets to your landline telephone system.

A drop cable carries the speech signal, a control signal and the ringing current into a master socket within the home. The phone signals are routed from the master socket to any extension sockets in the house in a line. Even though an extension cable normally has four wires, only three of these carry a signal to the terminals in the extension socket. See below for the correct terminal connections.

The four wires are colour coded. Blue with a white ring connects to terminal two, orange with a white ring to terminal three (the ringer terminal), and white with a blue ring to terminal five.

## MAINTENANCE

### EVERY SIX MONTHS

Check wiring *Make sure wiring fixed to skirting boards is not damaged. Also, check wiring run under doors is not crushed – re-route over doors if possible. Make sure connections into sockets are not loose, and that all socket faceplates are secure.*

## HOW MANY TELEPHONES ON THE LINE?

Every telephone and modem has a rating called the Ringer Equivalence Number (REN). On most telephones this number is one (it is usually found on the underside of the phone). A single telephone circuit can handle a maximum REN of four, or four standard-rated phones. Effectively, this is the total number of ringers that the electric current in the telephone cable can supply.

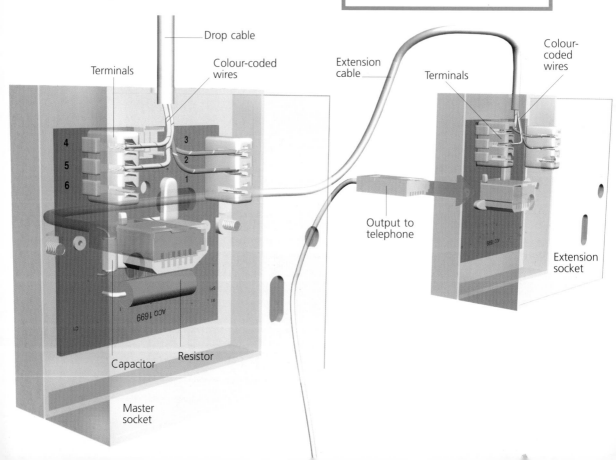

Drop cable

Terminals

Colour-coded wires

Extension cable

Terminals

Colour-coded wires

4
5
6

3
2
1

Output to telephone

Extension socket

Capacitor    Resistor

Master socket

## Wiring for home computers

If you subscribe to a broadband internet service you must fit an ADSL (Asymmetric Digital Subscriber Line) filter to every in-use telephone socket. The device is connected between the telephone socket and the computer modem, network router (below), telephone or digital satellite receiver (page 115) and splits the signal travelling along the telephone line into speech and digital communications. It allows you to use the internet and telephone at the same time.

Many homes now routinely have more than one computer. Linking them together in a network allows each one to share a single internet connection, printer, scanner or other device or to transfer files from one workstation to another easily. A 'peer-to-peer' network links computers in a line, like telephone extensions, but this primitive system cannot carry voice and data signals at the same time and the more computers that are placed on the line, the more the network signal is weakened.

A better option is to create a 'star' network, where computers are linked to a central hub or router. Network cables (see page 120) can be run below floorboards or hidden in the wall when a house is being built or replastered. A less disruptive option is to choose a wireless router that will transmit signals to wireless network cards installed in each workstation, but this may be slower than a hard-wired system.

The most powerful network cable, CAT5 data cable, allows you to run computer, telephone, music or audio-visual signals throughout the house, aswell as more sophisticated household electronics, such as intelligent lighting controls. It is worth considering installing a network if you are building or renovating a house.

## Checking the connections

Make sure that the wires are connected properly (see above). Note that some brands of cables do not have the standard colour-coding. In this case, follow the included instructions carefully.

### FAULT DIAGNOSIS

#### EXTENSION TELEPHONE NOT WORKING

Faulty sockets *Unplug converter from master socket and plug phone in directly. Try extension phone in extension socket. If neither phone works, call phone company. If all phones work, check the wiring in your extension socket and make sure the cable is not kinked or crushed. If one extension phone doesn't work, fault is likely to be with the phone.*

#### ONE OR MORE PHONES NOT RINGING PROPERLY OR AT ALL

Total REN of devices attached to phone line exceeds REN of main line (usually four) *Refer to manual for each device to check its REN value (see box opposite). Make sure total is within your telephone supplier's recommendation.*
Extension socket not connected correctly *Refer to wiring guides for correct connection.*

#### MODEM DOES NOT WORK

Wrong cable used *Modems sold for use in other countries sometimes use different connections within identical looking plugs and sockets. Make sure you are using the correct cable to work with the modem. Ask a reputable computer dealer for help if you are unsure.*

# Useful contacts

## Electricity

**Electrical Contractors Association**
ESCA House, 34 Palace Court
London W2 4HY
Tel: 020 7313 4800
Fax: 020 7221 7344
Email:
electricalcontractors@eca.co.uk
www.eca.co.uk

**National Inspection Council for Electrical Installation Inspecting (NICEIC)**
Warwick House
Houghton Hall Park
Houghton Regis
Dunstable
Bedfordshire LU5 5ZX
Consumer helpline: 0870 013 0382
Tel: 01582 531000
Fax: 01582 531010
Email: enquiries@niceic.com
www.niceic.org.uk

## Gas, Plumbing and Heating

**CORGI (Council for Registered Gas Installers)**
1 Elmwood
Chineham Park
Crockford Lane
Basingstoke RG24 8WG
Tel: 0870 401 2200
Fax: 0870 401 2600
Email: enquiries@corgi-group.com
www.corgi-group.com

**Association of Plumbing and Heating Contractors**
14 Ensign House
Ensign Business Centre
Westwood Way
Coventry CV4 8JA
Tel: 024 7647 0626
Fax: 024 7647 0942
Email: enquiries@aphc.co.uk
www.aphc.co.uk

**Institute of Plumbing and Heating Engineering**
64 Station Lane
Hornchurch
Essex
RM12 6NB
Tel: 01708 472791
Fax: 01708 448987
Email: info@iphe.org.uk
www.iphe.org.uk

## Security

**British Security Industry Association**
Security House
Barbourne Road
Worcester WR1 1RS
Tel: 01905 21464
Fax: 01905 613625
Email: info@bsia.co.uk
www.bsia.co.uk

**Master Locksmith's Association**
5D Great Central Way
Woodford Halse
Daventry NN11 3PZ
Tel: 0800 783 1498
Fax: 01327 262539
Email:
enquiries@locksmiths.co.uk
www.locksmiths.co.uk

## Decorating

**Painting and Decorating Association**
32 Coton Road
Nuneaton
Warwickshire CV11 5TW
Tel: 024 7635 3776
Fax: 024 7635 4513
Email: info@paintingdecorating association.co.uk
www.paintingdecorating association.co.uk

## Damp, rot and infestation

**British Wood Preserving and Damp-proofing Association**
1 Gleneagles House
Vernongate
South Street
Derby DE1 1UP
Tel: 01332 225100
Fax: 01332 225101
Email: info@bwpda.co.uk
www.bwpda.co.uk

**British Pest Control Association**
1 Gleneagles House
Vernongate
South Street
Derby DE1 1UP
Tel: 0870 609 2687
Fax: 01332 295904
Email: enquiry@bpca.org.uk
www.bpca.org.uk

## Advice on the internet

*There are many sites offering DIY and appliance repair advice on the internet. Many are linked to specific products or outlets and many are American sites, giving advice (particularly on plumbing and electrics) that does not conform to British safety standards. For impartial, UK-based advice, these are some of the best.*

**www.bbc.co.uk/homes/diy**
Very informative, with advice on most DIY jobs.

**www.diydoctor.org.uk/ home.htm**
Tips and tricks of the trade, information on products and details of local tradespeople and specialists.

**www.diyfixit.co.uk**
Information on general building, plumbing, electrics and more.

**www.easy-diy.co.uk**
A comprehensive site that offers advice on products and services.

**www.finddiy.co.uk**
An excellent starting point, with lots of links to other sites, plus information on tools, equipment and tradespeople.

**www.homepro.com**
Unusual style ideas as well as down-to-earth DIY, legal and financial advice and a guide to using contractors.

## A,B

alternating current (AC) 20
amplifier 104
amps 20
appliances
    disposal of 7
    faults 7
    warranties 7
    *see also individual appliances*
audio-visual connectors 110
ball floats 45
ballvalves 9, 31, 32, 43, 45
boilers 9, 32, 53
broadband 123
bulb, recessed, replacing 29

## C

cable detector 13, 16
cables
    circuit cables 23
    colour change 26
    earthing cable 23
    lighting cable 28
    service cables 22
    telephone cables 123
carbon monoxide detectors 17
cassette deck 102-103
CD player 100
central heating system 52-57
    boilers 9, 53
    components 9
    corrosion 9, 54
    draining 9
    faults 9, 56
    gravity-fed system 53
    leaks 56
    no heat/water 56
    pumped system 9, 52, 56
    sealed system 53
    *see also* radiators
circuit overload 23
cistern
    cold water cistern 31, 32
    feed-and-expansion cistern 9, 31, 52
    float valve, replacing 33
    jammed ballvalve 32
    toilet 31, 40, 41, 42
cleaning materials 14
computers
    connecting leads 120-121
    keyboard 116
    mouse 117
    printers 118-119
consumer unit 20, 22-23
cooker hood 26, 82-83
    fans 82, 83
    filters 82, 83
    noisy 83
cutting tools 10

## D

digital TV decoder 114-115
dishwasher 49, 77-79
    blocked valves 50
    cleaning 78
    loading 79
    poor washing performance 79
doorbells 61
drainage systems 48-51
    blockages 48, 49, 50, 51
    septic tanks 49
    single stack system 48
    traps and U-bends 48, 49, 50
    two-pipe system 48
DVD player 112-113

## E

ear defenders 15
earth connections 16
earthing cable 23
electric heaters, fan and radiant 94-95
electric kettle 86
electric shock 6, 16
electric shower 46-47
    descaling 46, 47
    leaking 47
    poor water flow 46, 47
    power shower 46, 47
    pressure 47
    pump filters 46, 47
    pump problems 47
    thermostat problems 47
electrical safety 16, 21, 28
electrical system 20-29
    circuits 20, 22
    consumer unit 22-23
    faults 6, 23
    lampholders 29
    on-off switch 23
    plugs 16, 20, 24-25
    socket outlets 20, 26-27
    switches 28-29
electrical tools 13
extractor fan 96-97

## F

fan heater 94, 95
filter coffeemaker 88
fire safety 17, 95
food processor 84-85
    blades, sharpening 85
    cleaning 84, 85
    non-functioning 85
fridge-freezer 7, 74-76
    cleaning 75
    defrosting 75, 76

(fridge-freezer, continued)
    moving 75
    thermostat problems 76
    frost thermostat 56
fused connection units (FCUs) 26
fuses and fuse wire 13, 16, 20, 22, 24
    blown fuse 6, 22, 25

## G,H

gas safety 9, 17
gloves 15
goggles 15
hard-water damage 35, 40, 42, 46, 87
header tank 9, 31, 52
hot water cylinder 31, 32, 58
    leaks 8

## I,K,L

immersion heater 32, 58-59
    element, replacing 59
    noisy 58
    sediment 58
    thermostat faults 58
insulating tape 13
iron 87
keyboard 116
ladders and steps 15
lampholder, replacing 29
lighting circuit 20, 28
locks
    cylinder locks 60-61
    key sticks 60, 63
    lubrication 60, 63
    mortise locks 62-63
loudspeaker 105

## M

measuring tools 12
meters 23, 30
microwave ovens 81
miniature circuit breakers (MCBs) 16, 22
    ratings 22
    tripped 6, 23, 25, 27
modems 121, 123
mouse (computer) 117
multimeter 13

## O

optical leads 110
outdoor power tools 16, 24
ovens and hobs 80-81
    cleaning 80

door problems 80, 81
gas hob 80
microwave ovens 81
timer/thermostat problems 81
uneven cooking 81

## P

pipes
    banging pipes 57
    blockages 8, 50
    frozen 32, 33, 56
    insulation 32, 54
    leaks 32
    waste pipes 8, 48, 50
    water supply pipes 8, 30
pliers 11
plugs 16, 20, 26
    faulty 25
    fitting 24-25
plumbing
    faults 8
    tools 12
plunger 12
power failure 6, 23
printers 118-119
PTFE tape 12
pumps
    central heating 9, 52, 53, 56
    showers 31, 47

## R

radiant heater 94, 95
radiators 9, 31
    banging 9
    bleeding 12, 54, 56
    leaks 9, 54, 55, 56, 57
RCA audio leads 110
record deck 101
remote control 111
residual current device (RCD) 13, 16, 22-23
ring main circuit 20
    spurs 20
rising main 8, 30, 43, 46

## S

safety
    electrical 16, 21, 28
    equipment 15
    fire 17, 95
    gas 9, 17
    in the home 16-17
SCART cables 110, 114, 115
screwdrivers 11
septic tanks 49
service cables 22

single-appliance circuit 20
smoke detectors 17
socket outlets 20, 26-27
    maximum load 16
    replacing 27
socket tester 13, 27
socket set 11
soil stack 48
spanners 12
spirit level 12
stilson wrench 12
stoptaps 8, 30, 31
storage tanks 8, 31
switches 28-29
    replacing 28

## T

taps 8, 34-39
    ceramic disc replacement 35, 39
    dripping 35, 37
    hard water damage 35
    leaking 34, 35
    mixer taps 38
    noisy 35
    O-rings 36, 38
    spindle taps 34, 35, 36-37
    stuck taps 35
    washer replacement 35, 37
telephone wiring 122-123
television 106-107
    cables and connections 106
    cathode ray tube (CRT) models 106
    cleaning 107
    digital TV decoder 114-115
    LCD models 106
    moving 106
    no picture/sound 107
    plasma screen models 106
    satellite television 114-115
    weak signal 107
toaster 89
toilets 40-45
    ballvalve problems 43, 45
    blockages 43, 44, 50
    bowl, levelling 44
    cisterns 31, 40, 41, 42
    continuous siphoning 43
    dual-flush system 41
    flushing problems 40, 43
    leaking 43
    limescale 40, 42, 43
    push-button cistern 41
    seat replacement 43
toolkit 10-15
traps and U-bends 48, 49, 50
tumble-dryer 71-73
    condenser dryer 71
    filters 72
    noisy 73
    poor drying performance 73
timer/thermostat faults 73

## V

vacuum cleaner 90-93
    bagless system 91, 92
    blockages 91
    brush roller problems 91, 93
    cylinder cleaner 90, 92
    drive belt 93
    filters 91, 92
    flex problems 93
    hybrid cleaner 90
    noisy 93
    poor suction 93
    upright cleaner 90, 93
ventilation regulations 97
video recorder 108-109
video signals 110
volts 20

## W

washing machine 49, 66-70
    blocked valves 50
    clothes damaged/still dirty 69
    detergent trays 67, 68
    door problems 67, 68, 69, 70
    drum problems 69
    filters and catchpots 67, 68
    flooding 67, 69
    inlet hoses 67
    leaking 69
    moving 70
    smells 50
    wash cycle problems 69
    water supply problems 69
waste pipes 8, 48, 50
    blocked 50, 51
    dismantling 50
waste water 48-51
water repellents 14
water system 30-33
    cold water supply 31
    direct systems 31, 32
    drinking water 31
    faults 32
    hot water supply 31-32
    indirect systems 31-32
    meters 30
    storage tanks 8, 31
    supply pipes 8, 30
    turning off the supply 31
    vented/unvented systems 31-32
watts 20
wire cutters and stripper 13

# Acknowledgments

All images in this book are copyright of the Reader's Digest Association Limited.

*Reader's Digest Household Maintenance & Repair Manual* is based on material in *How Everything in the Home Works* and *Reader's Digest DIY Manual* both published by The Reader's Digest Association Limited, London

First Edition Copyright © 2006
The Reader's Digest Association Limited,
11 Westferry Circus, Canary Wharf,
London E14 4HE
www.readersdigest.co.uk

**Editor** Alison Candlin
**Art Editor** Louise Turpin
**Assistant Editor** Celia Coyne
**Editorial Consultant** Mike Lawrence
**Proofreader** Ron Pankhurst
**Indexer** Marie Lorimer

**Reader's Digest General Books**
**Editorial Director** Cortina Butler
**Art Director** Nick Clark
**Executive Editor** Julian Browne
**Managing Editor** Alastair Holmes
**Picture Resource Manager** Martin Smith
**Pre-press Account Manager** Sandra Fuller
**Senior Production Controller** Deborah Trott
**Product Production Manager** Claudette Bramble

The Reader's Digest Association Limited would like to thank Graham Dixon for his technical advice in producing this book.

**Origination** Colour Systems Limited, London
**Printing and binding** Everbest Printing Co. Ltd, China

The contents of this book are believed to be accurate at the time of printing. However the publisher accepts no responsibility or liability for any work carried out in the absence of professional advice.

We are committed to both the quality of our products and the service we provide to our customers. We value your comments, so please feel free to contact us on 08705 113366, or via our website at www.readersdigest.co.uk
If you have any comments about the content of our books, email us at gbeditorial@readersdigest.co.uk

ISBN-13: 978 0276 44188 2
ISBN-10: 0 276 44188 5
BOOK CODE: 400-288-01
ORACLE CODE: 250003455H.00.24